LOW FAT
HIGH FLAVOUR

LOW FAT
HIGH FLAVOUR

Sonja Grey

hamlyn

First published in Great Britain in 1997 by
Hamlyn, a division of Octopus Publishing Group Ltd
2–4 Heron Quays, London E14 4JP

This edition published 2003 by Octopus Publishing Group Ltd

Reprinted 2004

Copyright © 1997, 2003 Octopus Publishing Group Ltd

ISBN 0 600 61116 7

Printed in China

NOTES

Both metric and imperial measurements have been given in
all recipes. Use one set of measurements only and not a
mixture of both.

Standard level spoon measurements are used in all recipes.
1 tablespoon = one 15 ml spoon
1 teaspoon = one 5 ml spoon

Eggs should be medium to large unless otherwise stated.
The Department of Health advises that eggs should not be
consumed raw. This book contains dishes made with raw or
lightly cooked eggs. It is prudent for more vulnerable people
such as pregnant and nursing mothers, invalids, the elderly,
babies and young children to avoid uncooked or lightly cooked
dishes made with eggs. Once prepared, these dishes should
be kept refrigerated and used promptly.

Meat and poultry should be cooked thoroughly. To test if
poultry is cooked, pierce the flesh through the thickest part
with a skewer or fork – the juices should run clear, never
pink or red. Do not re-freeze poultry that has been frozen
previously and thawed. Do not re-freeze a cooked dish that
has been frozen previously.

Milk should be full fat unless otherwise stated.

Nuts and Nut Derivatives.
This book includes dishes made with nuts and nut
derivatives. It is advisable for people with known allergic
reactions to nuts and nut derivatives and those who may be
potentially vulnerable to these allergies, such as pregnant and
nursing mothers, invalids, the elderly, babies and children, to
avoid dishes made with nuts and nut oils. It is also prudent to
check the labels of pre-prepared ingredients for the
possible inclusion of nut derivatives.

Pepper should be freshly ground black pepper unless
otherwise stated.

Fresh herbs should be used, unless otherwise stated. If
unavailable, use dried herbs as an alternative but halve the
quantities stated.

Measurements for canned food have been given as a standard
metric equivalent.

Ovens should be preheated to the specified temperature –
if using a fan-assisted oven, follow the manufacturer's
instructions for adjusting the time and the temperature.

Vegetarians should look for the 'V' symbol on a cheese to
ensure it is made with vegetarian rennet. There are vegetarian
forms of Parmesan, Feta, Cheddar, Cheshire, Red Leicester,
dolcelatte and many goats' cheeses, among others.

All the recipes in this book have been analysed by a
professional nutritionist, so that you can see their nutritional
content at a glance. The abbreviations are as follows:
Kcal = calories; KJ = kilojoules; CHO = carbohydrate. The
analysis refers to each portion. Use in conjunction with the chart
on page 7.

Contents

Introduction

Low Fat, High Flavour? – many of us who have grown up in the Western world would consider that statement to be a contradiction in terms. Red meat, butter, whole milk, cream, full fat cheese, all these have been a part of our daily lives. The post-war parent, relieved to be freed of wartime austerity, could not wait to be able to offer the good things that the nation's children had been denied for so long.

Our entire agricultural economy is based on the production and consumption of these products. But perhaps even more to the point our food culture with traditional recipes like roast beef and Yorkshire pudding, milk puddings and custards, our whole notion of wholesome delicious food is rooted in these foods. So what is wrong with that? Well, nothing in moderation, but the incidence of coronary heart disease has increased dramatically in the past fifty years and medical research has identified several major causes. Stress, that demon of the late 20th century, is one, lack of exercise and tobacco contribute, and too high a consumption of saturated fats and a high level of cholesterol in our diet is a factor too. Those saturated fats are present in the very foods we eat most, red meat and dairy products and

some oils like coconut and palm oil.

We need fat in a balanced diet to exist; it is essential to us but saturated fats are not essential in the quantities which we consume them. For one thing, too much fat in our diet increases our chances of obesity, which in turn adds to our risk of suffering heart disease.

Low Fat, High Flavour is not about giving up all the things we like to eat best, nor is it a faddy diet book; it is a collection of carefully planned recipes which allow us to monitor the fats we consume without compromising on taste. The recipes in this book have been devised and nutritionally analysed so that any cook can find inspiration for delicious meals which will also contribute to a healthier, leaner diet. Some

classic dishes have been made with dramatically reduced fat content, and you may find the portions rather smaller than usual. However, steamed vegetables have no fat at all and green salad without oil in the dressing can be heaped on to the plate. The salmon dish shown on the cover is a special treat, although dramatically reduced in fat it contains a slightly higher proportion of fats than the other main courses. We suggest you save it for a special occasion when you can limit your daily intake of fats at other meals. So what are the benefits of reducing our daily intake of fats? Well, besides reducing the risk of heart disease, when combined with a check on calories and an increase in other sources of proteins such as wholegrains and fresh vegetables and fruits, many people find that their weight is easier to control, particularly if they take regular exercise. Their general health and sense of wellbeing as well as resistance to infection can improve too.

Nowadays many of our foods are labelled with their carbohydrate, fat, protein and calorie content. It is a good idea to get into the habit of studying food labels so that it becomes easy to calculate a recommended daily intake of the main nutrient groups.

WHAT TO EAT AND HOW TO COOK IT

So what should we do to keep our daily intake of fats within these guidelines? Here is a brief guide to the main food groups and their value in our diet and some alternative methods for preparing and cooking them.

DAIRY PRODUCTS

One of the main sources of saturated fats is dairy products; whole milk, butter, cream, cheese and ice cream. Where possible reduce your intake of all fat. However, polyunsaturated fats, contained in margarine or safflower, sunflower, olive and rapeseed oils although weight for weight containing the same fat and calorie content as butter, are a healthier source of fat than dairy products. Try to replace whole milk with semi-skimmed or skimmed milk. Cream substitutes, based on polyunsaturated fats and low-fat ice creams can all contribute to lowering our intake of saturated fats. Natural yogurt and low-fat hard cheeses, cottage and curd cheeses can also help.

EGGS

One large egg yolk contains almost a whole day's recommended allowance of cholesterol, about 250–275 milligrams. It is a good idea to limit your intake of egg yolks to three a week. Egg whites contain no cholesterol and are a good source of protein. So, for example, if you are preparing scrambled eggs or omelettes, it is better to use one yolk and several whites to increase the portion size whilst limiting the cholesterol and fat intake.

BEEF, LAMB AND PORK

Watching your fat intake does not mean giving up all meat. But take care. Limit your portions to about 75 g/3 oz, look for lean cuts and remove all visible fats before cooking. Try to mince very lean steak like sirloin yourself or ask your butcher to do so. When roasting meats, always place a rack in the bottom of the roasting tin so that the meat does not sit in its own juices, and try to roast for longer, but at a lower temperature, 180° C (350° F), Gas Mark 4, so that meat is not seared, thus sealing in the fat. If you are grilling meat, try adding flavour by marinating it first in herbs, wine, tomato or lemon juice. Incidentally, if you casserole or stew meat it is a good idea to start the cooking off the day before. Chill the stew and skim off the solidified fat before completing the cooking time.

SAUSAGES AND PROCESSED MEATS

These product often have hidden fats so read the labels carefully and select those with no more than 10% fat by weight or three grammes of fat per ounce.

POULTRY AND GAME

These foods are often lower in fats than red meat but do be careful to choose

---

In general, as a rule of thumb, whatever your daily calorie intake, the recommended proportions of nutrients are as follows:

NUTRIENT	RECOMMENDED INTAKE
Total fat	35% of total energy (kcal) (e.g. in a 2000 calorie diet not more than 700 calories should come from fat. This equals 80 g fat per day, or 40 g fat for every 1000 calories)
Saturated fatty acids	Less than 10% of total energy (kcal)
Polyunsaturated fatty acids	Up to 10% of total energy (kcal)

NUTRIENT	RECOMMENDED INTAKE
Monounsaturated fatty acids	10–15% of total energy (kcal)
Carbohydrate	50% of total calories
Protein	10–20% of total calories
Total Calories	To achieve and maintain desirable weight

COOKING FISH IN A PARCEL
1 Cut out a double sheet of greaseproof paper or kitchen foil large enough to enclose the fish. Place the herbs and flavourings on the paper.

2 Sprinkle the cleaned fish inside and out with salt and pepper and place on the herb mixture on the greaseproof paper or foil.

3 Fold the paper over the fish and wrap loosely, securing the sides with a double fold and double folding the ends. Place on a baking sheet and cook in a preheated oven.

lean varieties. Chicken and turkey are leaner than goose and duck for example. Most of the fat in poultry is just beneath the skin so remove the skin and trim away all visible fat before cooking.

Poaching, sautéing, grilling and stir-frying are all good methods for cooking poultry and meat, needing little oil, provided they are cooked at high temperatures and kept moving in the wok or pan. Microwaving is also an excellent way to cook without adding extra fat. Indeed you can drain food of extra fat by placing it between two sheets of kitchen paper while it is cooking.

FISH AND SHELLFISH
Fish is often recommended as a good source of protein and is generally lower in cholesterol than red meat. Steaming or poaching and once again microwaving are all good methods of cooking fresh fish. Cooking whole fish in paper or foil

parcels with herbs and flavourings seals in the flavour without the need to add extra fat during cooking (see above). Shellfish: prawns, lobster, crab, and other shellfish are very low in fat although weight for weight some types of shellfish contain more cholesterol than meat and poultry. However, even these can be eaten occasionally.

FRUITS, VEGETABLES, GRAINS AND LEGUMES
These foods have no cholesterol and tend to be low in fat and often high in fibre and vitamins. Olives and avocados are high in fat but since the fat is largely unsaturated they need to be avoided only for their high calorie count. Be careful, however, to check the labels of processed foods made from vegetables, grains or legumes for fats added during processing. Breads and pastas made with egg yolks should be avoided. Also

check that processed vegetables have not had sodium added. Ideally, fresh produce is always a better choice.

NUTS AND SEEDS
Many people like to use these tasty foods as snacks, but they do tend to have high concentrations of fats and can be high in calories. Nuts and seeds do not contain cholesterol and their fats are normally unsaturated.

CAKES, PASTRIES, CRACKERS AND CRISPBREADS
Cakes and pastries tend to be high in calories and fat and not of any great food value. If you are baking at home, try to substitute oil for fat and egg whites for yolks. Read the labels on packets of crackers and crispbreads before buying as they are often coated in vegetable oil before crisping, and may be higher in fat than you imagine.

VEGETABLE STOCK

- 3 medium potatoes, peeled and chopped
- 1 medium onion, peeled and thinly sliced
- 2 leeks, split, cleaned and chopped
- 2 celery sticks, chopped
- 2 medium carrots, peeled and chopped
- 1 small fennel head, thinly sliced
- thyme, parsley stalks and 2 bay leaves
- salt and pepper

1 Put all the vegetables into a pan with the herbs and 1.5 litres/2½ pints water. Bring to the boil slowly, then skim.
2 Add salt and pepper to taste. Simmer for about 1½ hours, covered, skimming the stock three or four times during cooking.
3 Strain the stock through clean muslin or a very fine sieve. Cool quickly and store in the refrigerator until required.

Makes about 1 litre/1¾ pints

FISH STOCK

- 1 kg/2 lb fish trimmings
- 1 small onion, peeled and finely chopped
- 2 leeks, split, cleaned and chopped
- 1 bay leaf
- parsley stalks, sprigs of fennel and lemon rind
- 1.2 litres/2 pints water
- 200 ml/⅓ pint dry white wine
- salt and pepper

1 Place the fish trimmings in a large saucepan with the onion, leeks, bay leaf, parsley, fennel, lemon rind and water. Bring to the boil, slowly then skim any surface scum.

2 Add the white wine, and salt and pepper to taste and simmer very gently for 30 minutes, skimming the stock once or twice during cooking.
3 Strain the stock through clean muslin or a very fine sieve. Cool quickly and keep chilled until needed.

Makes about 1 litre/1¾ pints

LEMON YOGURT DRESSING

- 150g/5 oz natural yogurt
- 1 tablespoon lemon juice
- 2 teaspoons chopped mixed fresh herbs
- salt and pepper

Place all the ingredients in a bowl and whisk with a fork until well blended. Cover with clingfilm and chill in the refrigerator until ready to serve

**Kcal 35; KJ 145; Protein (9)
Fat (4) g; CHO 2 (g) per half quantity**

LEMON HERB SEASONING

- 4½ tablespoons dried basil
- 4 tablespoons dried oregano
- 1 tablespoon pepper
- 1½ tablespoons dried onion
- ½ tablespoon whole celery seeds
- ½ teaspoon grated lemon rind
- ½ teaspoon dried garlic

Place all the ingredients in bowl. Toss gently with spoon until well blended. Store in an airtight container in a cool dry dark place for up to 6 months.

Makes about 1 jar

SALSA

- 6 small ripe tomatoes, skinned and finely chopped
- 1–2 chilli peppers, cored, deseeded and finely chopped, or to taste
- 2 tablespoons finely chopped onion
- 2 tablespoons chopped fresh parsley
- 2 tablespoons fresh lime or lemon juice
- 2 teaspoons wine vinegar
- ⅛ teaspoon salt (optional)
- pepper, to taste

Place all ingredients in a food processor or blender and work until smooth.
Note: Always wear rubber gloves when handling chillies.

Serves 4–6

**Kcal 97; KJ 411; Protein 5 (g)
Fat 2 (g); CHO 16 (g)**

GUACAMOLE

- 1 avocado peeled, stoned and mashed
- 1 tablespoon fresh lime or lemon juice
- 1½ tablespoons Salsa (see above)
- 1 ripe tomato, skinned and chopped
- 2 tablespoons finely chopped onion
- 2 tablespoons chopped fresh coriander
- 1 garlic clove, finely chopped
- pepper

Mix together all ingredients in a bowl. Cover and chill until required.

Serves 8

**Kcal 42; KJ 174; Protein (9)
Fat (4) g; CHO 2 (g)**

Warm and Chilled Soups

Yellow Pepper Soup

Slightly sweet, yellow peppers are milder in flavour than green ones. All peppers are rich in vitamin C.

3 yellow peppers, cored and deseeded

50 g/2 oz butter or margarine

1 small onion, chopped

1.2 litres/2 pints Vegetable Stock (see page 9)

1 teaspoon mild curry powder

¼ teaspoon turmeric

1 tablespoon chopped fresh coriander, or

1 teaspoon dried leaf coriander

300 g/10 oz potatoes, peeled and chopped

salt

1 Chop one pepper finely and place it in a small saucepan, then chop the remaining peppers roughly.

2 Melt 25 g/1 oz of the butter or margarine in another saucepan and cook the onion and roughly chopped peppers for 5 minutes, stirring frequently. Stir in the stock, curry powder, turmeric and coriander, then add the potatoes. Bring to the boil, then lower the heat and simmer, partially covered, for 40–45 minutes, or until the vegetables are very soft.

3 Melt the remaining butter with the finely chopped pepper in the small pan. Cook over a gentle heat until the pepper is very soft. Reserve for the garnish.

4 Purée the onion, pepper and potato mixture in batches in a blender or food processor until very smooth. Return to a clean saucepan and reheat gently. Serve in heated soup plates or bowls, garnished with a little of the sautéed chopped pepper.

Serves 8

Preparation time: 15–20 minutes

Cooking time: 50–55 minutes

Kcal 100; KJ 425; Protein 2 (g); Fat 5 (g); CHO 11 (g)

Orange Consommé

A deliciously refreshing starter to any meal. The preparation takes hardly any time at all and, if you want to speed up the chilling process, cool and cover the consommé, then place it in the freezer until the surface is covered with a thin layer of ice.

- 1 x 475 g/15 oz can beef consommé
- juice of 3 oranges
- 2 cloves
- cayenne pepper, to taste
- 1 orange, sliced thinly, to garnish

1 Pour the consommé into a pan. Add the orange juice to the pan with the cloves and cayenne to taste. Bring the mixture to the boil, then remove the cloves, using a slotted spoon. Tip the contents of the pan into a bowl and set aside until cool.

2 When the orange consommé is cool, cover the surface closely and chill for 3–4 hours in the refrigerator. Alternatively freeze the mixture for about 30 minutes, until the surface is covered with a thin layer of ice.

3 Serve in chilled bowls, garnishing each portion with an orange slice.

Serves 6
Preparation time: 3–5 minutes, plus chilling
Cooking time: 3–5 minutes

**Kcal 35; KJ 150; Protein 3 (g)
Fat 0 (g); CHO 6 (g)**

Fennel Soup

- 2 fennel bulbs, with leaves
- 1 onion, finely chopped
- 600 ml/1 pint Chicken Stock (see page 14)
- 150 ml/¼ pint skimmed milk
- 1 teaspoon pesto
- salt and pepper
- small wholemeal croûtons, to serve

1 Remove the feathery leaves from the fennel, and reserve for a garnish. Cut the bulbs into shreds.

2 Put the fennel into a saucepan with the onion, chicken stock, skimmed milk and salt and pepper to taste. Bring to the boil and simmer gently for about 20 minutes until the fennel is just tender.

3 Purée the soup in a food processor or blender until smooth. Return to a clean saucepan, add the pesto and heat through over a low heat.

4 Ladle the hot soup into small bowls. Garnish with the fennel leaves, and serve with wholemeal croûtons.

Serves 4
Preparation time: 5 minutes
Cooking time: 20 minutes

**Kcal 70; KJ 280; Protein 4 (g)
Fat 2 (g); CHO 10 (g)**

Tomato, Orange and Tarragon Soup

Establish your culinary reputation with this! A refreshing soup that can be served hot or cold is a sure winner.

- 1 tablespoon vegetable oil
- 1 onion, sliced
- 175 g/6 oz potatoes, peeled and diced
- 1.75 kg/3½ lb tomatoes, chopped
- 2 tablespoons chopped fresh tarragon or 1 teaspoon dried tarragon
- 1 garlic clove, crushed
- 500 ml/17 fl oz Chicken Stock (see right)
- 250 ml/8 fl oz orange juice
- 1 teaspoon freshly grated orange rind
- sprigs of tarragon or parsley, to garnish
- ¼ teaspoon salt (optional)
- pepper, to taste

1 Heat the oil in a heavy saucepan over medium-high heat. Sauté the onions and potatoes for 2–3 minutes, or until the onions are translucent.
2 Add the tomatoes, tarragon, garlic, stock and salt and pepper. Bring to the boil, then reduce the heat and simmer, covered, for 20–25 minutes, or until the vegetables are tender.
3 Purée the soup in a blender or food processor, then pass through a sieve and discard the pulp that remains in the sieve.
4 Mix the orange juice and rind into the soup. Reheat or serve chilled, garnished with fresh tarragon or parsley sprigs, if liked.

Serves 8
Preparation time: 15 minutes
Cooking time: about 30 minutes

**Kcal 65; KJ 275; Protein 2 (g)
Fat 2 (g); CHO 10 (g)**

Chicken Stock

Put a 1.5 kg/3 lb chicken into a large saucepan with 2.4 litres/4 pints water and bring slowly to the boil. Remove any surface scum. Add a bouquet garni, 1 small onion peeled and stuck with 3 cloves, salt and pepper to taste and a small bunch of tarragon. Lower the heat and simmer gently for 1½ hours, skimming regularly. Strain the stock through fine muslin or a very fine strainer. Cool quickly and chill until required.

Makes 1 litre/1¾ pints

Chilled Watercress Soup

Watercress is pleasantly pungent and gives an almost peppery flavour to this cold soup.

- 1 tablespoon oil
- 1 onion, chopped
- 2 bunches of watercress, thick stems discarded, chopped coarsely
- 1 tablespoon flour
- 750 ml/1¼ pints Vegetable Stock (see page 9)
- 1 medium potato, cut into 1 cm/½ inch dice
- pinch of grated nutmeg
- 2 heaped tablespoons dried skimmed milk powder
- salt and pepper
- a few watercress leaves, to garnish
- 1 tablespoon olive oil (optional)

1 Heat the oil in a saucepan. Add the onion and watercress and cook over a moderate heat for 10 minutes, stirring frequently. Remove from the heat and stir in the flour. Return to the heat, stirring until thickened. Add the stock, potatoes and nutmeg, and salt and pepper to taste, bring to the boil, then lower the heat and simmer, covered, for 15–20 minutes, or until the potatoes are soft. Leave to cool slightly.
2 Purée the mixture in batches in a food processor or blender. Transfer to a large bowl, cover closely and chill in the refrigerator for at least 3 hours.
3 Just before serving, add the dried milk and blend until smooth. Taste and adjust the seasoning. Serve in chilled bowls, garnishing each portion with a few watercress leaves and a little olive oil, if using, and black pepper.

Serves 8
Preparation time: about 10 minutes, plus 3 hours chilling time
Cooking time: 25 minutes

**Kcal 60; KJ 246; Protein 3 (g)
Fat 2 (g); CHO 9 (g)**

Spinach Soup

Although frozen leaf spinach can be used for this recipe, the full-flavoured taste of fresh spinach cannot be matched.

- 25 g/1 oz butter or margarine
- 1 onion, chopped
- 250 g/8 oz fresh or frozen spinach, thawed if frozen
- 600 ml/1 pint Vegetable Stock (see page 9)
- 1 medium potato, peeled and thinly sliced
- 1 teaspoon lemon juice
- pinch of grated nutmeg
- 90 ml/3½ fl oz semi-skimmed milk
- salt and white pepper
- ground almonds, to garnish (optional)

1 Heat the oil in a heavy-based saucepan. Add the onion and cook over moderate heat until soft but not golden. Add the spinach and cook until soft, stirring constantly.

2 Pour the stock into the pan and add the potatoes, lemon juice and nutmeg and salt and pepper to taste. Cook, partially covered, over moderate heat for 10–12 minutes, or until the potatoes are soft.

3 Purée the mixture in a food processor or blender until smooth. Return to a clean saucepan. Add the milk and heat the soup gently without boiling. Transfer to heated soup bowls, sprinkling each portion with ground almonds, to garnish, if you like.

Serves 8

Preparation time: 10 minutes
Cooking time: about 20 minutes

**Kcal 67; KJ 279; Protein 4 (g)
Fat 3 (g); CHO 8 (g)**

Jerusalem Artichoke Soup

- 500 g/1 lb Jerusalem artichokes
- 3 tablespoons lemon juice
- 1 tablespoon sunflower oil
- 900 ml/1½ pints Chicken Stock (page 14)
- 1 teaspoon dried dill
- ½ teaspoon sugar
- salt and pepper

LEMON CROUTONS:

- 4 slices crustless bread
- 1 tablespoon lemon juice

1 Chop the artichokes into small pieces, sprinkling them liberally with lemon juice as you work.

2 Heat the oil in a saucepan and add the artichokes, stirring well. Cover and sweat over a gentle heat for 1–2 minutes. Pour on the stock, bring to the boil, cover and simmer for about 30 minutes.

3 Purée the artichokes in a food processor or blender with the dried dill and sugar, then push through a sieve and return to a clean pan. Reheat, and add salt and pepper to taste.

4 To make the lemon croûtons, brush both sides of the slices of bread with lemon juice and toast until lightly coloured on both sides. Cut into cubes.

5 Serve the soup garnished with croûtons.

Serves 4
Preparation time: 20 minutes
Cooking time: 45–50 minutes

**Kcal 150; KJ 690; Protein 5 (g)
Fat 4 (g); CHO 27 (g)**

Curried Parsnip Soup

- 375 g/12 oz parsnips, scraped and chopped
- 1 onion, chopped
- 600 ml/1 pint Chicken Stock (see page 14)
- 1 teaspoon mild curry powder
- salt and pepper

TO GARNISH:

- natural yogurt (optional)
- coriander leaves (optional)
- Melba toast, to serve

1 Place the parsnip and onion in a large saucepan with the stock and season with salt and pepper. Bring to the boil, cover and simmer for 20 minutes, or until the parsnips are tender.
2 Remove from the heat and allow to cool slightly, then purée in a blender or food processor, or press through a fine sieve, and stir in the curry powder.
3 Return the soup to a clean pan and reheat. Serve hot.

VARIATION

Curried Carrot Soup

Substitute carrots for the parsnips. Increase the quantity of curry powder if a hotter flavour is liked.

Serves 6
Preparation time: 15 minutes
Cooking time: about 30 minutes

**Kcal 90; KJ 385; Protein 3 (g)
Fat 2 (g); CHO 17 (g)**

Parsnip and Carrot Soup

- 250 g/8 oz parsnips, scraped and chopped
- 250 g/8 oz carrots, scraped and chopped
- 1 onion, chopped
- 600 ml/1 pint Chicken Stock (see page 14)
- salt and pepper
- natural yogurt, to garnish (optional)

1 Place the parsnips, carrots and onion in a large saucepan with the stock and season with salt and pepper. Bring to the boil, cover and simmer for 20 minutes, or until the vegetables are tender.
2 Remove from the heat and allow to cool slightly, then purée in a food processor or blender until smooth, or press through a fine sieve.
3 Return the soup to the cleaned pan and reheat. Serve hot in individual heated soup bowls, garnished with yogurt if liked.

Serves 4
Preparation time: 15 minutes
Cooking time: about 30 minutes

Kcal 70; Kj 298; Protein 3 (g); Fat 1 (g); CHO 14 (g)

Carrot and Sage Soup

Fresh sage is often unavailable during the winter months, but dried sage may be used instead. Soak it first in a tablespoon of warmed white wine.

- 25 g/1 oz butter
- 1 large onion, finely chopped
- 750 g/1½ lb carrots, finely sliced
- 900 ml/1½ pints Vegetable Stock (see page 9)
- 1 tablespoon chopped fresh sage
- salt and pepper
- sprigs of fresh sage, to garnish (optional)

1 Melt the butter in a large heavy-based pan, add the onion and gently fry until soft but not golden, then add the carrots and stock. Season with salt and pepper.
2 Bring to the boil and simmer uncovered for about 30 minutes.
3 Purée the soup in a food processor or blender until smooth, then return to a clean pan and add the chopped sage. Bring to the boil and simmer for another 15 minutes.
4 Serve garnished with sage sprigs.

Serves 6
Preparation time: 15 minutes
Cooking time: about 1 hour

**Kcal 87; KJ 360; Protein 2 (g)
Fat 4 (g); CHO 0 (g)**

Chilled Fresh Fruit Soup

On a sweltering summer's day this healthy concoction of fruit, juices and honey is an ideal replacement for breakfast, or even lunch.

- 2 dessert apples, peeled, quartered and cored
- 6 bananas, roughly chopped
- 500 g/1 lb fresh strawberries
- 375 g/12 oz pears, peeled, quartered and cored
- 1 litre/1¾ pints fresh orange juice
- 2 tablespoons lemon juice
- 300 ml/½ pint fresh grapefruit juice
- 5–6 tablespoons clear honey
- crushed black peppercorns or sprigs of fresh mint and strawberries, to garnish

1 Place all the fruit in a food processor or blender with 300 ml/½ pint of the orange juice and blend until very smooth. Add the lemon juice and grapefruit juice and the honey. Blend again until the mixture is smooth, in batches if necessary.

2 Pour the soup into a large bowl, stir in the remaining orange juice and cover the bowl loosely. Chill in the refrigerator for 3-4 hours.

3 Pour the chilled soup into 6 chilled bowls and garnish each portion with crushed black peppercorns or a sprig of fresh mint and a strawberry.

Serves 6
Preparation time: 10 minutes, plus chilling

**Kcal 290; KJ 1250; Protein 3 (g)
Fat 1 (g); CHO 73 (g)**

Chilled Tomato and Basil Soup

- 1 kg/2 lb ripe tomatoes, skinned, deseeded and chopped
- 1 large garlic clove, finely chopped
- 1 tablespoon chopped fresh basil
- 450 ml/¾ pint Chicken Stock (see page 14)
- juice of 1 large orange
- 2 anchovy fillets, chopped
- salt and pepper

PESTO CROUTES:

- 4 thin slices wholemeal bread
- 2 teaspoons pesto

1 Put the tomatoes into a large pan with the garlic, basil, stock, orange juice, anchovy fillets and salt and pepper to taste.
2 Bring to the boil and simmer for 3–4 minutes.
3 Cool slightly and then purée the mixture in a food processor or blender until smooth. Transfer to a large bowl, cover and chill for at least 4 hours.
4 To make the pesto croûtes, spread each slice of wholemeal bread with a thin layer of pesto. Place under a preheated grill until a light golden brown. Cut into fingers.

5 Ladle the soup into bowls and serve with the croûtes.

Serves 4
Preparation time: 15–20 minutes, plus chilling
Cooking time: 6–7 minutes

**Kcal 125; KJ 523; Protein 6 (g)
Fat 3 (g); CHO 20 (g)**

Low-fat Vichyssoise

This sophisticated iced soup is made from humble ingredients: leeks and potatoes. It was created in the 1920s by Louis Diat, a French chef working in the United States. Vichyssoise can be prepared 24 hours in advance and must always be velvety smooth and well chilled. The name, vichyssoise, is also given to any cold soup based on potato combined with another vegetable such as courgettes.

- 25 g/1 oz butter or margarine
- 1 kg/2 lb leeks, white part only, thinly sliced
- 1 onion, chopped
- 1 litre/1¾ pints Vegetable Stock (see page 9)
- pinch of grated nutmeg
- 750 g/1½ lb old potatoes, peeled and cubed
- 900 ml/1½ pints semi-skimmed milk
- salt and white pepper
- 2 tablespoons snipped fresh chives, to garnish

1 Melt the butter or margarine in a pan. Add the leeks and onion and cook over moderate heat for 5 minutes, stirring constantly. Do not allow the vegetables to change colour.
2 Add the stock, nutmeg and potatoes with salt and pepper to taste. Bring the mixture to the boil, lower the heat and cook, partially covered, for 25 minutes. Pour in the milk and simmer for 5–8 minutes more. Cool slightly.

3 Purée the mixture in batches in a food processor or blender until smooth, then rub it through a sieve into a bowl. Stir well and cover the bowl closely. Chill in the refrigerator for at least 3 hours. Just before serving, adjust the seasoning, adding more salt and pepper if required. Serve in chilled bowls, garnishing each portion with a generous sprinkling of snipped chives.

Serves 8

Preparation time: 15 minutes, plus chilling
Cooking time: about 35 minutes

**Kcal 180; KJ 758; Protein 8 (g)
Fat 5 (g); CHO 27 (g)**

Avgolemono

This is a simple but effective way of preparing the delicious egg and lemon soup from Greece.

- 1.5 litres/2½ pints Chicken Stock (see page 14)
- 50 g/2 oz white long-grain rice
- 2 eggs
- 2–3 tablespoons lemon juice
- 1 tablespoon chopped fresh parsley (optional)
- salt and pepper

1 Combine the stock, ½ teaspoon of salt and the rice in a saucepan. Bring the mixture to the boil. Stir, lower the heat, cover the pan and simmer for 20 minutes. Stir once more.

2 Beat the eggs in a small bowl, then whisk in the lemon juice. Add a ladleful of stock, beat, and then add another ladleful of stock and beat once more.

3 Bring the remaining stock and rice mixture back to the boil. Briefly remove the saucepan from the heat and add the egg and lemon mixture.

Stir well, lower the heat and simmer for a further 2 minutes, adding salt and pepper to taste. Sprinkle in the parsley, if using. Serve at once in heated bowls.

Serves 6
Preparation time: about 10 minutes
Cooking time: 25 minutes

**Kcal 60; KJ 255; Protein 4 (g)
Fat 2 (g); CHO 7 (g)**

Cream of Celery and Prawn Soup

This fragrant, smooth soup may be served hot or chilled and takes only a few minutes to prepare

- 1 x 300 g/10 oz can condensed cream of celery soup
- 300 ml/½ pint semi-skimmed milk
- ½ teaspoon paprika
- ½ teaspoon white pepper
- 2 tablespoons very low fat natural yogurt
- 50 g/2 oz cooked peeled prawns, defrosted if frozen (optional)
- snipped fresh chives, to garnish

1 Mix the celery soup and milk in a saucepan. Add the paprika a little at a time, to taste, and white pepper. Bring to simmering point, stirring constantly, for 5 minutes, then take the pan off the heat.

2 If serving the soup hot, stir in the yogurt and prawns, if using, and reheat gently for about 2 minutes. Do not boil. Serve in heated bowls, garnishing each portion with snipped chives.

3 If serving the soup chilled, pour the soup into a bowl and leave to cool. Stir in the yogurt and prawns, cover the bowl and chill for at least 3 hours. Serve the soup in chilled bowls, garnishing each portion with snipped chives.

Serves 6
Preparation time: 3–5 minutes, plus chilling
Cooking time, if serving cold: 5 minutes

Kcal 100; KJ 425; Protein 2 (g); Fat 5 (g); CHO 11 (g)

Basil and Potato Soup

- 15 g/½ oz butter
- 750 g/1½ lb floury potatoes, peeled and grated
- 6 garlic cloves, peeled
- 50 g/2 oz fresh basil, chopped
- 600 ml/1 pint Chicken Stock (see page 14)
- 600 ml/1 pint dry white wine
- 1 teaspoon lemon juice
- salt and pepper

1 Heat the butter in a large heavy-based saucepan and add the potatoes, garlic and half of the basil. Stir over a gentle heat for a couple of minutes, then add the stock and wine.
2 Bring to the boil and cook uncovered for 15 minutes, until all the potatoes are quite soft.
3 Purée the soup in a food processor or blender until smooth, adding the remaining basil at the same time.
4 Taste and add lemon juice, salt and pepper if needed; if the soup is to be served chilled the seasoning will need to be more pronounced.
5 Chill thoroughly and serve.

Serves 6
Preparation time: 10 minutes, plus chilling
Cooking time: 20 minutes

**Kcal 187; KJ 787; Protein 4 (g)
Fat 2 (g); CHO 23 (g)**

Red Lentil Soup

- 250 g/8 oz split red lentils
- 1 leek, sliced
- 2 large carrots, sliced
- 1 celery stick, sliced
- 1 garlic clove, crushed (optional)
- 1 bay leaf

- 1.2 litres/2 pints Vegetable Stock (see page 9)
- ½ teaspoon cayenne pepper
- pepper

TO GARNISH:

- very low-fat natural yogurt
- snipped fresh chives or finely chopped fresh parsley

1 Place all the ingredients except the garnish in a large saucepan, bring to the boil, cover and simmer for 20–25 minutes or until the lentils and all the vegetables are tender.

2 Allow the soup to cool slightly and remove the bay leaf. Purée the soup in batches in a food processor or blender until smooth.

3 Return the soup to a clean saucepan, season with pepper, and heat through. To serve, transfer to heated soup plates or bowls, garnishing each portion with a swirl of yogurt and a sprinkling of chives or parsley.

Serves 4
Preparation time: 10 minutes
Cooking time: 25–30 minutes

**Kcal 140; KJ 600; Protein 10 (g)
Fat 1 (g); CHO 25 (g)**

Vegetable and Pasta Soup

- 250 g/8 oz carrots, diced
- 250 g/8 oz courgettes, sliced
- 2 large celery stalks, chopped
- 1 large onion, finely chopped
- 125 g/4 oz cabbage, shredded
- 600 ml/1 pint Chicken Stock (see page 14)
- 300 ml/½ pint tomato juice
- 1 garlic clove, crushed
- 125 g/4 oz small pasta shapes
- salt and pepper

1 Place all the vegetables in a saucepan with the stock, tomato juice and garlic. Bring to the boil, then reduce the heat, skim off the scum that rises to the surface and add the pasta. Season with salt and pepper, cover and simmer for 15–20 minutes or until all the vegetables and the pasta are tender.
2 Serve piping hot in warmed individual soup bowls.

Serves 4
Preparation time: 15 minutes
Cooking time: about 25 minutes

**Kcal 150; KJ 630; Protein 6 (g)
Fat 1 (g); CHO 30 (g)**

Minestrone Soup

- 125 g/4 oz haricot beans, soaked overnight
- 1 tablespoon vegetable oil
- 2 onions, chopped
- 2 garlic cloves, crushed
- 1.8 litres/3 pints water
- 1 teaspoon chopped fresh marjoram
- ½ teaspoon chopped fresh thyme
- 4 tomatoes, skinned, deseeded and chopped
- 2 carrots, diced
- 2 potatoes, diced
- 1 small turnip, diced
- 1–2 celery sticks, chopped
- 250 g/8 oz cabbage, shredded
- 50 g/2 oz small pasta shapes
- 1 tablespoon chopped fresh parsley
- salt and pepper
- 3 tablespoons grated Parmesan cheese, plus extra to serve

1 Drain the beans and rinse under running cold water.

2 Heat the oil in a large saucepan and add the onions and garlic. Sauté gently for about 5 minutes, stirring occasionally, until soft and golden brown.

3 Add the beans, water, herbs and tomatoes, cover the pan and simmer gently for 2 hours. Add the carrots and simmer for 10 minutes. Stir in the potatoes and turnip and cook for another 10 minutes.

4 Add the celery and cabbage to the soup with the pasta shapes and cook for 10 minutes, or until the pasta and all the vegetables are tender. Add the parsley and season to taste. Stir in the Parmesan and then ladle into individual soup bowls. Serve immediately with extra Parmesan cheese.

Serves 8
Preparation time: 20 minutes, plus soaking overnight
Cooking time: 2½ hours

Kcal 140; KJ 580; Protein 7 (g)
Fat 4 (g); CHO 20 (g)

Main
Courses

Spaghetti with Three Herb Sauce

3 tablespoons chopped fresh parsley
1 tablespoon chopped fresh tarragon
2 tablespoons chopped fresh basil
1 tablespoon olive oil
1 large garlic clove, crushed
4 tablespoons Chicken Stock (see page 14)
2 tablespoons dry white wine
375 g/12 oz multi-coloured spaghetti
salt
pepper

1 Put the parsley, tarragon, basil, olive oil, garlic, chicken stock, white wine and salt and pepper to taste into a food processor or blender and work until smooth.
2 Cook the spaghetti in a large pan of boiling salted water for 10–12 minutes until just tender.
3 Drain the spaghetti and heap in a warmed bowl; pour over the herb sauce and toss well, then serve immediately.

Serves 4
Preparation time: 15 minutes
Cooking time: 10–12 minutes

Kcal 317; KJ 1343; Protein 12 (g); Fat 5 (g); CHO 58 (g)

Chicken and Pasta Twist Bake

- 600 ml/1 pint skimmed milk
- 40 g/1½ oz plain flour, sieved
- pepper
- 200 g/7 oz tri-colour pasta twists
- 250 g/8 oz boneless, skinless chicken breast, cooked and diced
- 50 g/2 oz fresh wholemeal breadcrumbs

1 Place the milk and flour in a saucepan and bring to the boil over gentle heat, stirring constantly until the sauce thickens. Simmer for 1 further minute, stirring frequently, then season generously with pepper.
2 Meanwhile, cook the pasta twists in a large pan of boiling water according to the manufacturer's instructions until just tender. Drain well.
3 Stir the chicken into the sauce and pour into a 2.4 litre/4 pint shallow ovenproof dish. Spoon the pasta twists over the sauce, pressing them in lightly, without submerging them completely. Sprinkle the breadcrumbs over the top of the pasta and bake in a preheated oven, 190°C (375° F), Gas Mark 5, for about 20 minutes until the breadcrumbs are golden and crisp. Serve hot.

Serves 4
Preparation time: about 15 minutes
Cooking time: about 20 minutes
Oven temperature: 190°C (375°F), Gas Mark 5

Kcal 380; KJ 1597; Protein 28 (g) Fat 3 (g); CHO 63 (g)

Tagliatelle with Tomato Sauce

- 2 tablespoons olive oil, plus extra for cooking pasta
- 2 onions, chopped
- 2 garlic cloves, crushed
- 500 g/1 lb plum tomatoes, skinned and chopped
- 2 tablespoons tomato purée
- 1 teaspoon sugar
- 125 ml/4 fl oz dry white wine
- a few ripe olives, stoned and quartered
- a handful of torn basil leaves
- 250 g/8 oz dried tagliatelle
- 25 g/1 oz grated Parmesan cheese (optional)
- salt and pepper

1 Heat 1 tablespoon of the olive oil in a large frying pan. Add the onions and garlic, and sauté gently over low heat until they are tender and slightly coloured. Stir the mixture occasionally.

2 Add the tomatoes and tomato purée together with the sugar and wine, stirring well. Cook over gentle heat until the mixture is quite thick and reduced. Stir in the olives and basil leaves and season to taste with salt and plenty of pepper.

3 Meanwhile, add the tagliatelle to a large pan of boiling salted water (to which a little oil has been added to prevent the pasta sticking). Boil rapidly until the tagliatelle is *al dente*.

4 Drain the tagliatelle immediately, mixing in the remaining olive oil and a generous grinding of pepper. Arrange the pasta on 4 serving plates and top with the tomato sauce, mixing it into the tagliatelle. Serve sprinkled with Parmesan cheese, if liked.

Serves 6
Preparation time: 10 minutes
Cooking time: 20 minutes

Kcal 220; KJ 940; Protein 6 (g)
Fat 5 (g); CHO 38 (g) (no Parmesan)

Peperonata with Wholemeal Noodles

Peperonata is a classic summer dish, combining the best of summer produce – peppers, fresh tomatoes and fresh basil. Use fresh wholemeal noodles if you can – these take about 8–10 minutes to cook, but the extra time is well worth it for the flavour.

- 2 tablespoons olive oil
- 1 large onion, thinly sliced
- 1 large garlic clove, crushed
- 2 red peppers, cored, deseeded and cut into strips
- 2 green peppers, cored, deseeded and cut into strips
- 375 g/12 oz tomatoes, skinned, deseeded and chopped
- 1 tablespoon chopped fresh basil
- 175 g/6 oz wholemeal noodles
- salt and pepper
- sprigs of fresh basil, to garnish (optional)

1 Heat 1 tablespoon of the olive oil in a deep frying pan. Add the onion and garlic and cook very gently until the onion is soft but not coloured. Add the peppers, tomatoes, basil and salt and pepper to taste. Cover and cook gently for 10 minutes.

2 Remove the lid from the pan and cook over fairly high heat until most of the moisture has evaporated. Keep the vegetable mixture warm.

3 Meanwhile, cook the noodles in plenty of boiling salted water until just tender. Drain the noodles thoroughly and toss in the remaining olive oil. Add salt and pepper to taste.

4 Divide the noodles among 4 serving plates and spoon the hot peperonata over the top. Garnish with sprigs of fresh basil and serve immediately, as a light main course with a salad.

Serves 6
Preparation time: 20–25 minutes
Cooking time: 20 minutes

**Kcal 170; KJ 720; Protein 6 (g)
Fat 5 (g); CHO 28 (g)**

Chicken Véronique

- 4 skinless chicken breasts, weighing
  150 g/5 oz each
- 300 ml/½ pint Chicken Stock (see page 14)
- 15 g/½ oz cornflour
- 175 ml/6 fl oz skimmed milk
- 200 g/7 oz skinless green grapes, halved
- salt and pepper

1 Trim any visible fat away from the chicken breasts. Place the chicken breasts in a heavy-based frying pan, pour over the stock and bring to the boil. Cover the pan and simmer gently for 20 minutes or until the chicken breasts are thoroughly cooked.

2 Remove the chicken breasts from the pan with a slotted spoon and keep warm. Strain the stock through a fine sieve into a measuring jug. Wipe the frying pan clean with kitchen paper and return 150 ml/¼ pint of the stock to the clean pan.

3 Blend the cornflour with a little of the milk then add to the stock in the pan with the remaining milk. Bring to the boil over moderate heat, stirring constantly. When the sauce has thickened, return the chicken breasts to the pan, add the halved grapes and simmer for 5 minutes until the chicken and grapes are heated through. Season to taste, then serve immediately.

Serves 4
Preparation time: 20 minutes
Cooking time: 30 minutes

**Kcal 230; KJ 966; Protein 35 (g)
Fat 5 (g); CHO 13 (g)**

Baked Trout Parcels

- 2 garlic cloves, crushed
- 1 onion, chopped
- 1 celery stick, chopped
- 4 sprigs of fresh rosemary
- 2 tablespoons dry white wine
- 2 x 200 g/7 oz trout, cleaned
- salt and pepper
- sprigs of rosemary, to garnish

1 Put the vegetables in the top part of a steamer. Steam gently for about 5 minutes until soft and tender. Season with salt and pepper, add 2 of the rosemary sprigs and the dry white wine and cook gently for 5 minutes.

2 Cut out 2 double sheets of kitchen foil or greaseproof paper large enough to enclose the trout. Divide the onion mixture equally between the 2 pieces of paper.

3 Wash the trout and dry well with kitchen paper. Sprinkle inside and out with salt and pepper. Place one trout on top of the onion mixture on each piece of foil or paper and top with a sprig of rosemary.

4 Fold the foil or paper over the fish and wrap loosely, securing the sides with a double fold and double folding the ends. Place the parcels on a baking sheet and cook in a preheated oven, 180°C (350°F), Gas Mark 4, for 20 minutes or until the fish is cooked and tender. Remove the fish from the foil or paper and serve garnished with sprigs of rosemary.

Serves 2
Preparation time: 10–15 minutes
Cooking time: 20 minutes
Oven temperature: 180°C (350°F), Gas Mark 4

Kcal 150; KJ 624; Protein 22 (g); Fat 4 (g); CHO 4 (g)

VARIATION

Baked Trout Parcels with Dill and Watercress

Cook the garlic and onion as for the main recipe. Replace the celery with 50 g/2 oz chopped watercress and substitute fresh dill for the sprigs of rosemary. Follow the main recipe and serve garnished with watercress.

Trout in a Paper Bag

- 4 small trout, about 125 g/4 oz each, cleaned
- 2 garlic cloves, finely chopped
- 1 tablespoon chopped fresh thyme
- 1 tablespoon chopped fresh rosemary
- 150 ml/¼ pint rosé wine
- salt and pepper

1 Cut 8 rectangles of greaseproof paper or kitchen foil, double the width of each trout, and half as long again as the fish.

2 Place 4 of the rectangles on a baking sheet. Lay a trout along the centre of each one, pull up the edges of the paper or foil and fold at each corner so that the paper forms a container for each fish.

3 Sprinkle a little salt and pepper, garlic and herbs over each trout, then spoon 2 tablespoons of the rosé wine over each one. Cover loosely with the remaining paper or foil and fold at the corners as before to form a lid over each fish. Fold the top and bottom layers of paper or foil together in several places. Bake the trout in a preheated oven, 190°C (375°F), Gas Mark 5,

for 35–40 minutes, until the fish is cooked.

4 Take the fish to the table in the parcels to serve.

Serves 4
Preparation time: 30 minutes
Cooking time: 35–40 minutes
Oven temperature: 190°C (375°F), Gas Mark 5

**Kcal 160; KJ 680; Protein 23 (g)
Fat 5 (g); CHO 1 (g)**

Hoki with Light Lemon Sauce

Hoki is available at good fishmongers and larger supermarkets, although other white fish such as cod or haddock could be used instead.

- **4 x 175 g/6 oz hoki fillets**
- **150 ml/¼ pint cold water**
- **2 teaspoons cornflour**
- **150 ml/¼ pint skimmed milk**
- **100 g/4 oz very-low-fat natural yogurt**
- **2 teaspoons lemon juice**
- **grated rind of 1 lemon**
- **½ teaspoon granular low-calorie sweetener**
- **sprigs of parsley, to garnish**

1 Place the hoki fillets in a large frying pan with the cold water and bring to the boil over gentle heat. Simmer for 5–10 minutes, depending on the thickness of the fish. The fish will be fully cooked when the flesh turns white and flakes when gently pressed. Using a fish slice, transfer the cooked fish to a warm serving dish, cover and keep warm.

2 While the fish is cooking, blend the cornflour with the milk and place in a small saucepan. Bring to the boil, stirring constantly, to make a smooth, thick sauce. Reduce the heat and simmer gently for 3–4 minutes to cook the cornflour thoroughly, stirring from time to time.

3 Remove the sauce from the heat and carefully stir in the yogurt, lemon juice, half of the lemon rind and the low-calorie sweetener. Return to the heat to warm through, but do not allow the sauce to boil.

4 To serve, pour the warm sauce over the hoki fillets. Garnish with the remaining lemon rind and the sprigs of parsley.

Serves 4
Preparation time: 20 minutes
Cooking time: 15 minutes

**Kcal 190; KJ 798; Protein 34 (g)
Fat 2 (g); CHO 42 (g)**

Poached Salmon Steaks with Hot Basil Sauce

- 1 large bunch of fresh basil
- 2 celery sticks, chopped
- 1 carrot, chopped
- 1 small courgette, chopped
- 1 small onion, chopped
- 4 salmon steaks, about 50 g/2 oz each and
  1 cm/½ inch thick
- 75 ml/3 fl oz white wine
- 125 ml/4 fl oz water
- 1 teaspoon lemon juice
- 15 g/½ oz unsalted butter
- salt and pepper

1 Strip the leaves off half the basil and set aside.

2 Spread the chopped celery, carrot, courgette and onion evenly over the bottom of a large flameproof dish or pan with a lid, place the salmon steaks on top and cover them with the remaining basil.

3 Pour over the wine and water and add salt and pepper to taste. Bring to the boil, cover and simmer for about 10 minutes. Transfer the salmon to a warmed serving dish.

4 Bring the poaching liquid and vegetables back to the boil and simmer for 5 minutes. Strain into a blender or food processor and add the cooked and uncooked basil. Blend to a purée and transfer to a saucepan.

5. Bring the purée to the boil and reduce by half, until thickened.

6 Remove the pan from the heat, add

the lemon juice and stir in the butter. Pour the sauce over the salmon steaks and serve.

Serves 4

Preparation time: 20 minutes
Cooking time: 45–50 minutes

**Kcal 170; KJ 710; Protein 12 (g)
Fat 11 (g); CHO 4 (g)**

Piquant Plaice

- 8 small plaice fillets, skinned, about 50 g/ 2 oz each
- ¼ teaspoon ground ginger
- 1 small onion, finely chopped
- 150 ml/¼ pint white wine
- 150 ml/¼ pint Chicken Stock (see page 14)
- 2 leeks, cut into matchstick strips
- 4 tablespoons very-low-fat natural yogurt
- 1 thin slice fresh root ginger
- ½ teaspoon mild curry powder
- salt and pepper
- small croûtons, to garnish

1 Lay the plaice fillets skinned sides uppermost and sprinkle with salt, pepper and ginger. Roll up and secure with wooden cocktail sticks.

3 Scatter the onion in a large frying pan, lay the plaice on top and add the white wine and stock. Cover the pan and simmer gently for about 10 minutes. Remove the plaice paupiettes with a slotted spoon and keep warm.

3 Meanwhile, simmer the strips of leek in boiling water for 3 minutes, then drain.

4 Put the yogurt into a bowl. Squeeze the ginger in a garlic press to extract the juice and add to the yogurt with the curry powder and seasoning.

5 Arrange 2 paupiettes on each plate and garnish with the strips of leek and croûtons. Serve the sauce separately.

Serves 4
Preparation time: 20 minutes
Cooking time: 13 minutes

**Kcal 185; KI 784; Protein 23 (g)
Fat 3 (g); CHO 11 (g)**

Sole and Smoked Salmon Paupiettes

- 6 small sole fillets, about 50 g/2 oz each, skinned
- 4 slices smoked salmon, about 25 g/1 oz
- 1 tablespoon chopped dill
- 300 ml/½ pint fish stock
- 300 ml/½ pint Herb and Lemon Sauce (see right) (optional)
- 50 g/2 oz cooked, peeled prawns
- salt and pepper

TO GARNISH:
- sprigs of fresh dill
- twists of lemon

1 Lay the sole fillets out flat and season with salt and pepper. Cut the slices of smoked salmon in half lengthways and lay a strip down the length of each sole fillet. Sprinkle with chopped dill and roll up loosely. Secure with wooden cocktail sticks.
2 Place the fish rolls in a shallow pan and add the fish stock. It should cover the fish. Cover and simmer for about 8 minutes until just tender. Drain the fish and keep warm on a serving dish.
3 Spoon 4 tablespoons of the fish cooking liquid into a small pan and boil quickly over a high heat until reduced to about 1 tablespoon.
4 Stir the Herb and Lemon Sauce, if using, and the prawns into the reduced cooking liquid and heat through gently. Spoon the sauce evenly over the fish paupiettes and garnish with sprigs of fresh dill and twists of lemon.

Serves 6
Preparation time: 15 minutes
Cooking time: about 8 minutes

Kcal 114; KJ 480; Protein 23 (g)
Fat 2 (g); CHO 0 (g)

Herb and Lemon Sauce

- 2 hard-boiled egg yolks
- grated rind and juice of 1 lemon
- 1 teaspoon French mustard
- 1 teaspoon soft dark brown sugar
- 4 tablespoons Vegetable Stock (see page 9)
- 2 tablespoons olive oil
- 4 tablespoons yogurt
- 1 tablespoon each finely chopped fresh tarragon, basil and parsley
- salt and pepper

1 Mix the egg yolks to a paste with the lemon rind and juice, mustard and sugar.
2 Gradually beat in the chicken stock, olive oil and yogurt.
3 Add the herbs, and salt and pepper to taste.

Makes about 300 ml/½ pint
Preparation time: 10 minutes

(For recipe with sauce)
Kcal 185; KJ 777; Protein 26 (g)
Fat 8 (g); CHO 3 (g)

Fillets of Sole with Melon and Mint Sauce

- 4 fillets of sole, halved
- 2 tablespoons chopped mint
- 300 ml/½ pint dry white wine
- 1 Charentais melon, halved and seeded
- 150 ml/¼ pint natural yogurt
- salt and pepper
- sprigs of fresh mint, to garnish

1 Season the sole fillets with salt and pepper and sprinkle with half of the mint. Roll up each fish fillet and secure with wooden cocktail sticks. Place the fish rolls in a deep frying pan and sprinkle over the remaining mint. Add the white wine. Cover the pan and poach gently for about 8 minutes, until the fish is tender.

2 Meanwhile, using a Parisian cutter or melon ball cutter, scoop the melon flesh into small balls. Cut out any remaining melon flesh attached to the skin.

3 Carefully drain the rolled fillets, place on a warm serving dish and keep warm. Remove the cocktail sticks.

4 Boil the poaching liquid with the remnants of melon flesh until well reduced and whisk until smooth. If necessary, purée in a food processor or blender.

5 Stir in the yogurt and heat the sauce through gently. Season with salt and pepper and spoon over the cooked fish. Garnish with the melon balls and sprigs of mint.

Serves 4
Preparation time: 20 minutes
Cooking time: 10–12 minutes

**Kcal 230; KJ 985; Protein 29 (g)
Fat 3 (g); CHO 12 (g)**

Lemon Chicken

- 1 tablespoon olive oil
- 1 small onion, thinly sliced
- 4 chicken breasts, about 75 g/3 oz each, skinned and boned
- 2 tablespoons chopped fresh parsley
- 300 ml/½ pint Chicken Stock (see page 14)
- 1 tablespoon clear honey
- juice of 1 lemon
- rind of 1 lemon, cut into matchstick strips
- 2 teaspoons cornflour
- 1 tablespoon water
- salt and pepper

1 Heat the oil in a large frying pan. Add the onion and fry gently for 3–4 minutes. Add the chicken breasts and fry until lightly browned all over.

2 Add the parsley, stock, honey, salt and pepper to taste and lemon juice. Cover the pan and simmer gently for 20 minutes.

3 Using a slotted spoon remove the chicken breasts to a warmed serving dish, and keep warm.

4 Blend the cornflour and water to a smooth paste, stir in the hot cooking liquid, and then return to the pan. Stir over gentle heat until thickened. Add the strips of rind to the sauce and spoon evenly over the chicken.

Serves 4
Preparation time: 15 minutes
Cooking time: 30–35 minutes

Kcal 150; KJ 630; Protein 17 (g)
Fat 5 (g); CHO 9 (g)

Chicken Olives with Orange and Nut Stuffing

- 4 chicken breasts, about 75 g/3 oz each skinned, boned and halved
- finely grated rind of 1 orange
- 4 tablespoons fresh wholemeal breadcrumbs
- 1 small onion, finely chopped
- 2 tablespoons chopped fresh rosemary
- 1 tablespoon chopped walnuts
- 1 egg white
- 150 ml/¼ pint Chicken Stock (see page 14)
- 150 ml/¼ pint fresh orange juice
- salt and pepper

TO GARNISH:

- sprigs of fresh rosemary
- peeled orange segments

1 Lay the chicken breasts between dampened sheets of greaseproof paper and beat gently with a meat mallet or rolling pin.

2 Mix the orange rind with the breadcrumbs, onion, rosemary, walnuts and salt and pepper to taste and bind together with the egg white. Spread the mixture evenly over each chicken breast. Roll up securely and tie with strong cotton or fine string. Put the chicken olives in a shallow pan and add the stock and orange juice. Cover, bring to the boil and simmer for 25–30 minutes until the chicken is just tender.

3 Remove the chicken olives with a slotted spoon and keep warm on a serving dish. Remove the strings. Boil the cooking liquid until reduced by half. Spoon the cooking liquid over the chicken olives and garnish with rosemary sprigs and orange segments.

Serves 6
Preparation time: 20 minutes
Cooking time: 30–35 minutes

Kcal 140; KJ 590; Protein 14 (g); Fat 5(g); CHO 11 (g)

VARIATION

Chicken Olives with Lemon, Sage and Walnut Stuffing

Prepare the chicken breasts as for the main recipe. Mix the finely grated rind of 2 lemons with the breadcrumbs, onion, 1 tablespoon of chopped fresh sage, the walnuts and salt and pepper to taste and bind together with the egg white. Continue as for the main recipe, substituting 150 ml/½ pint lemon juice for the orange juice. Serve garnished with fresh sage and lemon wedges.

Serves 6
Preparation time: 20 minutes
Cooking time: 30–35 minutes

Kcal 133; KJ 560; Protein 14 (g) Fat 5 (g); CHO 9 (g)

Coq-au-vin

- 4 chicken pieces, about 175 g/6 oz each
- 4 tablespoons brandy
- 250 g/8 oz button onions, peeled
- 900 ml/1½ pints Chicken Stock (see page 14)
- 250 g/8 oz button mushrooms
- chopped fresh parsley, to garnish

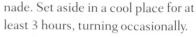
MARINADE:

- 1 garlic clove, crushed
- 150 ml/¼ pint red wine vinegar
- 150 ml/¼ pint red wine
- 1 tablespoon Worcestershire sauce
- salt and pepper

1 Combine all the marinade ingredients. Place the chicken in a large shallow bowl and pour over the marinade. Set aside in a cool place for at least 3 hours, turning occasionally.
2 Preheat the grill to high. Drain the chicken, reserving the marinade, and brown briefly under the grill. Transfer the pieces to a casserole.
3 Pour the brandy over the chicken and ignite. When the flames die down add the onions and stock. Cover and cook in the preheated oven, 220°C (425°F), Gas Mark 7, for 50 minutes.
4 Add the mushrooms and cook for 10 minutes, or until the chicken is tender and the juices run clear when pierced on the thickest part.
5 Meanwhile, pour the reserved marinade into a saucepan and boil rapidly, uncovered, until reduced by half. Stir into the casserole. Garnish with the chopped parsley and serve at once.

Serves 4
Preparation time: 10 minutes, plus marinating
Cooking time: about 1 hour
Oven temperature: 220°C (425°F), Gas Mark 7

**Kcal 190; KJ 790; Protein 19 (g)
Fat 4 (g); CHO 6 (g)**

Chicken Tandoori

- 4 chicken breasts, skinned, about 125 g/ 4 oz each
- 1 garlic clove, crushed
- 1 tablespoon tandoori powder
- 300 ml/½ pint very low fat natural yogurt
- onion slices, to garnish

1 Make incisions in the chicken flesh and rub with the garlic. Place the chicken in a large shallow bowl. Mix the tandoori powder with the yogurt and toss the chicken in the mixture. Place in the refrigerator to marinate for 3 hours.

2 Heat the grill to moderate. Remove the chicken from the marinade and place on the grill rack. Grill for about 20 minutes or until the chicken is cooked through, turning frequently and basting with the marinade.

3 Transfer the chicken to a heated serving dish, garnish with onion slices and serve immediately.

Serves 4
Preparation time: 5 minutes, plus marinating
Cooking time: about 20 minutes

**Kcal 190; KJ 800; Protein 31 (g)
Fat 5 (g); CHO 6 (g)**

Chicken Fajitas

This delicious dish is fun to make and good for you, too. Enjoy it with shredded lettuce, sliced tomatoes, Salsa and Guacamole (both on page 9) if you like.

- 625 g/1¼ lb boneless chicken breasts, skinned and cut into thin strips
- 2 teaspoons vegetable oil
- 1 large onion, cut into thin strips
- 1 large green pepper, cored, deseeded and cut into thin strips
- 8 flour tortillas

MARINADE:

- 1 garlic clove, finely chopped
- 1 tablespoon vegetable oil
- 1½ tablespoons fresh lemon or lime juice
- 3 tablespoons Worcestershire sauce
- ⅛ teaspoon pepper, or to taste

1 To make the marinade, combine the garlic, oil, lemon juice, Worcestershire sauce and pepper in a bowl. Add the chicken, toss to coat evenly and leave in the refrigerator for 10–20 minutes, turning at least once.
2 Heat the oil in a frying pan over medium-high heat. Add the onion and green pepper and sauté stirring constantly, for about 5 minutes, or until the onion is slightly brown. Remove and keep warm.
3 Wrap the tortillas in foil and place on the lower shelf of a preheated oven.
4 Line the grill pan with foil. Place the chicken strips on the foil and grill about 7 cm/3 inches from the heat for 4 minutes, turning once.
5 To serve, place 3 chicken strips on each tortilla and top with the onions, green peppers and assorted garnishes as desired. Roll the tortilla around the chicken strips and eat it with your fingers.

Serves 6

Preparation time: 15 minutes, plus marinating
Cooking time: about 10 minutes
Oven temperature: 200°C (400°F), Gas Mark 6

Kcal 300; KJ 1270; Protein 29 (g) Fat 5 (g); CHO 34 (g)

1 Put the turkey cubes into a shallow dish. Mix the lemon rind with the onion, garlic, pesto sauce, Basil and Garlic Oil, and salt and pepper to taste. Stir into the turkey, cover and chill for 3–4 hours.

2 Drain the turkey, reserving the marinade. Wrap each piece of turkey in a strip of Parma ham. Thread the turkey and ham rolls on kebab skewers, alternating with the mushrooms, bay leaves and wedges of lemon.

3 Brush the threaded skewers with the reserved marinade. Grill for 4–5 minutes. Turn the kebab skewers, brush once again with the marinade, and grill for a further 4–5 minutes.

4 Serve piping hot on a bed of shredded lettuce.

Serves 4
Preparation time: 20 minutes, plus chilling
Cooking time: about 10 minutes

**Kcal 187; KJ 788; Protein 33 (g)
Fat 5 (g); CHO 2 (g)**

Turkey and Parma Ham Kebabs

- 500 g/1 lb turkey fillet, cut into 4 cm/ 1½ inch cubes
- grated rind of 1 lemon
- 1 small onion, finely chopped
- 1 garlic clove, finely chopped
- 1 teaspoon pesto
- 1 tablespoon Basil and Garlic Oil (see right)
- 75 g/3 oz Parma ham, cut into long strips
- 8 small button mushrooms
- 8 small bay leaves
- 8 wedges of lemon
- salt and pepper
- shredded lettuce, to serve

Basil and Garlic Oil

Peel 4 large garlic cloves and bruise them with the back of a spoon. Put them into a bottle with 2 tablespoons chopped basil, 1 teaspoon black peppercorns and 600 ml/1 pint extra virgin olive oil. Firmly secure the bottle with a stopper and shake well. Store the oil in a cool place for 1 week before using.

Makes 600ml/1 pint

Pork Fillet with Grapefruit Sauce

- 250 g/8 oz pork fillet, cut into 5 mm/¼ inch thick medallions
- 3 spring onions, finely chopped
- finely grated rind and juice of ½ grapefruit
- 1 teaspoon soft light brown sugar
- 2 tablespoons chopped fresh parsley
- 1 tablespoon olive oil
- 150 ml/¼ pint unsweetened apple purée
- 150 ml/¼ pint Chicken Stock (see page 14)
- 2 grapefruit, peeled and divided into segments, pith and membrane removed
- salt and pepper

1 Place the pork medallions in a shallow dish with the spring onions, grapefruit rind and juice, brown sugar, salt and pepper to taste, and the parsley. Turn to coat well. Cover and chill for 3–4 hours.

2 Drain the pork medallions, reserving the marinade. Heat the oil in a frying pan and fry the medallions briskly until sealed on all sides.

3 Mix the apple purée with the stock and reserved marinade and pour over the pork. Cover and simmer for about 7 minutes until the pork is tender. Stir in the grapefruit segments and heat through.

Serves 6
Preparation time: 15 minutes, plus chilling
Cooking time: about 10 minutes

**Kcal 100; KJ 430; Protein 8 (g)
Fat 4 (g); CHO 9 (g)**

Pork Casserole

- 375 g/12 oz lean pork, diced
- 1 onion, sliced
- 150 g/5 oz carrot, sliced
- 500 g/1 lb baby new potatoes
- 400 ml/14 fl oz pork stock
- 2 bay leaves
- 100 g/4 oz frozen peas
- 75 g/3 oz green beans, trimmed
- 25 g/1 oz cornflour
- 50 ml/2 fl oz cold water
- pepper

1 Trim away any visible fat from the pork. Place the meat in a saucepan with the onion, carrot, potatoes, stock and bay leaves. Bring to the boil, cover and simmer for about 30 minutes, or until the meat is tender.

2 Add the peas and beans. Blend the cornflour with the water and stir into the casserole. Bring back to the boil, then cover and simmer for a further 5 minutes, stirring occasionally.

3 To serve, remove the bay leaves and season the casserole with a grinding of pepper.

Serves 4
Preparation time: 10 minutes
Cooking time: 35–40 minutes

**Kcal 290; KJ 1247; Protein 27 (g)
Fat 5 (g); CHO 35 (g)**

Apple Pork Chops

- 4 lean boneless pork loin chops, about 100 g/4 oz each
- 1 onion, sliced
- 200 ml/7 fl oz unsweetened clear apple juice
- 2 teaspoons chopped fresh thyme

- 2 cooking apples
- 2 tablespoons lemon juice
- 15 g/½ oz cornflour
- 2 tablespoons cold water
- pepper

1 Trim away any visible fat from the pork chops. Place the chops in a large heavy-based frying pan with the onion, apple juice and thyme. Bring the apple juice to the boil, cover the pan with a lid and simmer gently for about
15 minutes, then turn the chops over and simmer for a further 15 minutes or until the meat is fully cooked.
2 Meanwhile, core and peel the apples. Cut them into 5 mm/¼ inch slices and toss in the lemon juice to prevent browning.
3 When the pork is cooked, add the apple slices and cook for a further 5 minutes. Blend the cornflour with the water and stir well into the apple juice to thicken the sauce. Simmer for 1–2 minutes or until the apples are just tender. Do not overcook or the apples will lose their texture and shape and spoil the look of the dish.

Serves 4
Preparation time: 15 minutes
Cooking time: about 40 minutes

Kcal 220; KJ 946; Protein 23 (g)
Fat 5 (g); CHO 21 (g)

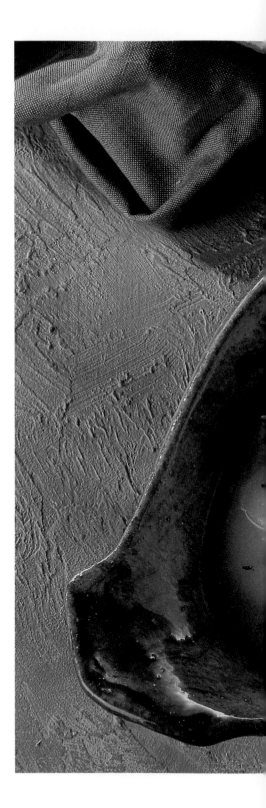

Stir-Fried Beef with Peppers

- 1 tablespoon olive oil
- 1 onion, thinly sliced
- 1 large garlic clove, cut into thin strips
- 450 g/1 lb fillet steak, cut into thin strips
- 1 red pepper, cored, deseeded and cut into matchstick strips
- 1 green pepper, cored, deseeded and cut into matchstick strips
- 1 tablespoon soy sauce
- 2 tablespoons dry sherry
- 1 tablespoon chopped fresh rosemary
- salt and pepper
- brown rice, to serve

1 Heat the olive oil in a wok or deep frying pan and stir-fry the onion and garlic for 2 minutes.
2 Add the strips of beef and stir-fry briskly until evenly browned on all sides and almost tender.
3 Add the strips of red and green pepper and stir-fry for a further 2 minutes.
4 Add the soy sauce, sherry, salt and pepper to taste and the rosemary, and stir-fry for a further 1–2 minutes. Serve piping hot with brown rice.

Serves 6
Preparation time: 5 minutes
Cooking time: 10–12 minutes

**Kcal 130; KJ 550; Protein 16 (g)
Fat 5 (g); CHO 3 (g)**

Sirloin Steaks with Tomato-garlic Sauce

- 4 sirloin steaks, about 50 g/2 oz each, trimmed
- 2 teaspoons low-fat spread

TOMATO-GARLIC SAUCE:

- 750 g/1½ lb tomatoes, skinned and chopped
- 3 garlic cloves, crushed
- 1 tablespoon chopped fresh basil
- salt and pepper
- sprigs of fresh basil, to garnish
- French beans, to serve

1 Heat the grill to high. Beat the steaks with a meat mallet or rolling pin until fairly thin, then spread with the low-fat spread. Place the steaks on the grill rack and grill for 8–10 minutes, or until cooked to your liking, turning them once.

2 Meanwhile, make the sauce. Place the tomatoes, garlic, basil and salt and pepper in a saucepan and simmer gently for about 10 minutes, until the tomatoes are soft.

3 Transfer the steaks to a heated serving dish and pour over the sauce. Serve immediately, garnished with the basil. Serve with French beans.

Serves 4
Preparation time: 10 minutes
Cooking time: about 20 minutes

**Kcal 140; KJ 590; Protein 15 (g)
Fat 5 (g); CHO 6 (g)**

Pheasant with Green Peppercorns

- 2 medium pheasants
- 175 ml/6 fl oz orange juice
- 1 garlic clove, peeled and crushed
- 1 tablespoon chopped chives
- 2 teaspoons green peppercorns
- 150 ml/¼ pint dry white wine
- 8 canned artichoke hearts
- salt

TO GARNISH:

- heart-shaped croûtons
- peeled orange segments

1 Using a very sharp knife, remove the breasts and drumsticks from each bird. Skin the birds, trimming any visible fat.
2 Put the pheasants into a dish with the orange juice, garlic, chives and salt. Cover and chill for 4 hours.
3 Transfer the pheasants and marinade to a frying pan. Add the peppercorns and the white wine and simmer for 15–20 minutes.
4 Add the artichoke hearts and simmer for a further 6–8 minutes, until the pheasants are just tender.
5 Remove the pheasants and artichoke hearts from the pan and keep warm.

6 Reduce the cooking juices slightly over a brisk heat; spoon over the pheasants and garnish with the croûtons and orange segments.

Serves 8
Preparation time: 20–25 minutes, plus chilling
Cooking time: about 30 minutes

**Kcal 180; KJ 750; Protein 20 (g)
Fat 5 (g); CHO 10 (g)**

Moussaka

- 750 g/1½ lb aubergines
- 2 teaspoons sunflower oil
- 1 large onion, chopped
- 1 tablespoon cornflour
- 300 ml/½ pint very low-fat natural yogurt
- 375 g/12 oz ripe tomatoes, skinned and chopped
- ½ teaspoon ground cinnamon
- 25 g/1 oz grated Parmesan
- 1 egg, plus 1 egg white, beaten
- salt and pepper

1 Slice two thirds of the aubergines 1 cm/½ inch thick, sprinkle them with salt and set them aside to drain.

2 Prick the rest of the aubergines all over and boil whole in salted water for 10 minutes.

3 Pat the sliced aubergines dry, paint each slice scantily with oil and grill until lightly coloured. Drain.

4 Poach the onion in a little water and cook gently until soft. Mix the cornflour into the yogurt.

5 Peel the whole aubergines and mash them, mix with the onions, tomatoes, 2 tablespoons of the yogurt mixture, salt, pepper and cinnamon.

6 Line an ovenproof dish with the sliced aubergines. Spread some of the mashed aubergines over the top and sprinkle with Parmesan. Repeat until the dish is nearly full.

7 Beat the egg mixture into the remaining yogurt and pour over, sprinkle with a little cinnamon and salt and bake in a preheated oven, 200°C (400°F), Gas Mark 6, for 20 minutes.

Serves 6

Preparation time: 45 minutes, plus draining
Cooking time: about 1 hour
Oven temperature: 200°C (400°F), Gas Mark 6

**Kcal 194; KJ 820; Protein 12 (g)
Fat 5 (g); CHO 23 (g)**

Stuffed Peppers

- 300 ml/½ pint water
- ½ teaspoon salt
- 175 g/6 oz brown rice
- 4 tomatoes, skinned and chopped
- 1 onion, grated
- 25 g/1 oz seedless raisins
- 75 g/3 oz low-fat Cheddar cheese, grated
- 2 tablespoons chopped fresh parsley
- pinch of ground cinnamon
- 4 green or red peppers, cored and deseeded, with tops reserved
- 5 tablespoons Chicken Stock (see page 14)
- pepper

1 Bring the water to the boil with the salt, add the rice and cook for 30 minutes, until the rice is tender and all the water has been absorbed.

2 When the rice is cooked, remove from the heat and gently stir in the tomatoes, onion and raisins. Stir in two-thirds of the cheese, then the parsley, cinnamon and pepper.

3 Cut a thin slice off the bottom of each pepper if necessary so that they will stand upright. Place the peppers upright in an ovenproof dish.

4 Divide the rice mixture equally among the peppers, sprinkle the remaining cheese over the tops and cover with the lids. Pour the stock around the peppers and cover with foil. Bake in the preheated oven, 200°C (400° F), Gas Mark 6, for 30–40 minutes, or until tender.

Serves 4
Preparation time: 35 minutes
Cooking time: 30–40 minutes
Oven temperature: 200°C (400° F), Gas Mark 6

**K cal 315; KJ 1330; Protein 12 (g)
Fat 5 (g); CHO 59 (g)**

Vegetable Hot-pot

- 4 carrots, sliced
- 4 parsnips, sliced
- 2 large courgette, sliced
- 2 turnips, sliced
- 2 red or green peppers, cored, deseeded and coarsely chopped
- 2 onions, sliced
- 2 large tomatoes, peeled, deseeded and chopped
- 600 ml/1 pint Chicken Stock (see page 14)
- 1 bay leaf
- 1 tablespoon chopped fresh parsley
- 1 teaspoon chopped fresh thyme
- 1 teaspoon chopped fresh marjoram
- a dash of Worcestershire sauce
- salt and pepper

1 Place all the ingredients in a flame-proof casserole. Bring to the boil, skim off the scum, then cover and cook gently for about 25 minutes, until all the vegetables are tender. Serve the hotpot immediately.

Serves 4
Preparation time: 10 minutes
Cooking time: about 25 minutes

**Kcal 166; KJ 700; Protein 6 (g)
Fat 2 (g); CHO 32 (g)**

Vegetable and Side Dishes

Caponata

3 aubergines cut into 1.25 cm/½ inch dice

2 tablespoons olive oil

1 onion, thinly sliced

2 celery sticks, diced

150 ml/¼ pint passata

3 tablespoons wine vinegar

1 yellow pepper, cored, deseeded and thinly sliced

1 red pepper, cored, deseeded and thinly sliced

25 g/1 oz anchovy fillets, soaked in warm water, drained and dried

50 g/2 oz capers, roughly chopped

25 g/1 oz black olives, pitted and sliced

25 g/1 oz green olives, pitted and sliced

salt

2 tablespoons chopped parsley, to serve

1 Put the diced aubergines into a colander, sprinkle with salt and leave to drain for 15–20 minutes to exude their bitter juices. Rinse under running cold water to remove any salt and pat dry with kitchen paper.

2 Heat the oil in a saucepan, add the onion and sauté until soft and golden. Add the celery and cook for 2–3 minutes. Add the aubergine and cook gently for 3 minutes, stirring occasionally. Add the passata and cook gently until it has been absorbed. Add the wine vinegar and cook for 1 minute. Add the peppers, anchovies, capers and olives and cook for 3 minutes.

3 Transfer the mixture to an ovenproof dish and bake, covered, in a preheated oven, 180°C (350°F), Gas Mark 4, for about 1 hour. Serve lukewarm or cold sprinkled with chopped parsley.

Serves 6

Preparation time: 40 minutes

Cooking time: 1 hour

Oven temperature: 180°C (350°F), Gas Mark 4

Kcal 74; KJ 313; Protein 3 (g); Fat 4 (g); CHO 7 (g)

Stir-fried Vegetables

- 1 tablespoon vegetable oil
- 125 g/4 oz bamboo shoots, thinly sliced
- 50 g/2 oz mangetout
- 125 g/4 oz carrots, thinly sliced
- 50 g/2 oz broccoli florets
- 125 g/4 oz fresh bean sprouts, rinsed
- 1 teaspoon each salt and sugar
- 1 tablespoon stock or water

1 Heat the oil in a preheated wok or frying pan. Add the bamboo shoots, mangetout, carrots and broccoli florets and stir-fry for about 1 minute.
2 Add the bean sprouts with the salt and sugar. Stir-fry for another minute or so, then add some stock or water if necessary. Do not overcook or the vegetables will lose their crunchiness. Serve hot.

Serves 4
Preparation time: 15–20 minutes
Cooking time: 3–5 minutes

**Kcal 68; KJ 280; Protein 3 (g)
Fat 3 (g); CHO 7 (g)**

Celeriac and Carrot Remoulade

- 1 celeriac root, about 250 g/8 oz, sliced into matchstick strips
- 2 tablespoons lemon juice
- 250 g/8 oz carrots, sliced into matchstick strips
- salt

DRESSING:

- 4 tablespoons low-fat mayonnaise
- 150 ml/¼ pint very low fat natural yogurt
- 1 garlic clove, crushed
- 1 tablespoon chopped fresh parsley
- 1 tablespoon finely snipped fresh chives
- ½ teaspoon mustard powder
- pinch of cayenne pepper

TO GARNISH:

- 1 hard-boiled egg, chopped
- snipped fresh chives
- carrot curls

1 Drop the celeriac strips as you cut them into a bowl of water with 1 tablespoon of the lemon juice.

2 Partly cook the celeriac and carrot strips for 5–8 minutes in boiling salted water with the remaining lemon juice. Drain, dry on kitchen paper and leave to cool.

3 To make the dressing, mix the ingredients in a bowl. Taste and adjust the seasoning if necessary.

4 Toss the celeriac and carrots in the dressing and spoon the salad on to a serving dish. Garnish with the hard-boiled egg, chives and carrot curls and serve.

Serves 4 as a side salad
Preparation time: 20 minutes, plus cooling
Cooking time: 10 minutes

**Kcal 94; KJ 390; Protein 4 (g)
Fat 4 (g); CHO 11 (g)**

Scalloped Potatoes

- 2 teaspoons vegetable oil
- 75 ml/3 fl oz low-fat soured cream
- 350 ml/12 fl oz skimmed milk
- 25 g/1 oz low-fat spread
- 1 tablespoon cornflour
- ⅛ teaspoon pepper
- 4 medium potatoes, about 750 g/1½ lb, cut into 5 mm/¼ inch slices
- ½ medium onion, diced
- paprika, to taste
- sprigs of thyme, to serve

1 Brush a rectangular 20 cm/8 inch x 12 cm/5 inch baking dish with oil.

2 In a medium bowl, whisk together the soured cream, skimmed milk, low-fat spread, cornflour and pepper.

3 Line the dish with one-third of the potato slices. Pour one-third of the soured cream mixture over the potatoes. Sprinkle half of the onion over the soured cream mixture. Repeat the layers in order: one-third of the potatoes, one-third of the soured cream mixture and the remaining onion. Arrange the remaining potatoes on the top and pour the remaining soured cream mixture over the top. Cover with foil and bake in a preheated oven, 180°C (350°F), Gas Mark 4, for 1 hour. Remove the foil and bake for a further 20 minutes.

4 Sprinkle with paprika and thyme sprigs, then let stand for 5 minutes before serving.

Serves 6
Preparation time: 20 minutes
Cooking time: 1 hour 20 minutes
Oven temperature: 180°C (350°F), Gas Mark 4

Kcal 185; KJ 777; Protein 5 (g) Fat 5 (g); CHO 30 (g)

Honey Carrots

Carrots prepared this way will be a favourite – even among the young ones in your family.

- 125 ml/4 fl oz water
- 750 g/1½ lb baby carrots, fresh or frozen
- 1 tablespoon margarine
- ½ tablespoon soft light brown sugar
- 2 tablespoons honey
- 2–3 tablespoons finely chopped fresh parsley

1 Pour the water into a medium saucepan. Add the carrots and bring to the boil. Reduce the heat, cover and simmer about 10 minutes, or until the carrots are tender-crisp. Drain. If using frozen carrots, follow packet directions for cooking.

2 Melt the margarine in a frying pan over medium-high heat. Add the sugar, honey and carrots. Reduce the heat and turn the carrots frequently for 1–2 minutes until well glazed. Sprinkle with parsley before serving.

Serves 6

Preparation time: 10 minutes
Cooking time: 12 minutes

**Kcal 87; KJ 365; Protein 1 (g)
Fat 3 (g); CHO 16 (g)**

Chilled Stuffed Artichokes

- 4 artichokes, stem trimmed and top third of leaves removed
- 1 tablespoon fresh lemon juice
- Steamed Vegetables with Ginger (see right)

SAUCE:

- 150 g/5 oz tofu, drained
- 4 tablespoons tomato purée
- 4 tablespoons horseradish sauce
- 2 teaspoons fresh lemon juice
- 2 teaspoons white vinegar
- ½ teaspoon Lemon Herb Seasoning (see page 9)
- ½ teaspoon onion salt
- ½ teaspoon sugar
- few drops Tabasco sauce
- freshly ground white pepper, to taste

1 Place the artichokes and lemon juice in a deep saucepan and add boiling water to cover. Cover and cook for 30 minutes, or until one of the other artichoke leaves pulls off easily. Remove from the pan, turn upside down to drain, then refrigerate to cool.
2 Remove the central choke of each artichoke and fill with chilled Steamed Vegetables with Ginger.
3 To make the sauce, place all the ingredients in a blender or food processor and purée. Pour some sauce over each artichoke to serve.

Serves 4
Preparation time: 20 minutes
Cooking time: about 35 minutes

Kcal 133; KJ 558; Protein 9 (g) Fat 3 (g); CHO 17 (g) (whole recipe)

Steamed Vegetables with Ginger

- 3 carrots, cut into 5 mm/¼ inch rounds
- 4 tablespoons tomato purée
- 75 g/3 oz cauliflower florets
- 75 g/3 oz broccoli florets
- 2 small courgettes, cut into 1 cm/½ inch rounds
- 3.5 cm/1½ inch piece root ginger, cut into thin strips

Place all the vegetables in a medium saucepan with the ginger and steam for 7 minutes until tender.

Serves 8
Preparation time: 10 minutes
Cooking time: 7 minutes

Duck and Mango Salad

- 3 x 175 g/6 oz duck breasts, boned
- 1 bunch of spring onions, cut into 2.5 cm/ 1 inch lengths
- 1 celery stick, chopped
- 1 teaspoon grated orange rind
- 500 g/1 lb brown rice, cooked
- 3 medium ripe mangoes, peeled and sliced
- salt and pepper

SAUCE:

- 1 egg white
- 1 whole egg
- 1 teaspoon Dijon mustard
- 1 tablespoon mango chutney
- ½ tablespoon soy sauce
- 1 tablespoon light vinegar, preferably a fruit vinegar
- 250 ml/8 fl oz natural very low fat yogurt

1 Arrange the duck breasts, skin-side up, on a rack and roast in a preheated oven for 10 minutes on each side.
2 Leave to cool, then remove the skin and cube the meat.
3 Meanwhile, make the sauce. Place the egg white, whole egg, mustard, mango chutney, soy sauce and vinegar in a food processor or blender and blend well, then add the yogurt, a tablespoon at a time.
4 Combine the duck meat with the onions, celery, orange rind, cooked rice and seasoning in a large bowl.
5 Arrange the mango slices on top of the salad and serve, accompanied by the sauce.

Serves 6
Preparation time: 25 minutes, plus cooling
Cooking time: 20 minutes
Oven temperature: 230°C (450°F), Gas Mark 8

Kcal 386; KJ 1640; Protein 16 (g) Fat 5 (g); CHO 72 (g)

Smoked Chicken and Fruit Salad

- 1 lettuce, shredded
- 2 celery sticks, chopped
- 1 red pepper, cored, deseeded and sliced
- 25 g/1 oz walnut halves
- 75 g/3 oz green grapes, peeled, halved and seeded
- 1 pear, peeled, cored and sliced
- 250 g/8 oz smoked chicken, skinned, boned and cut into strips or cubes

YOGURT AND CUCUMBER DRESSING:

- 2 tablespoons low-fat natural yogurt
- 2 tablespoons low-fat mayonnaise
- 2 tablespoons grated cucumber
- 1 teaspoon grated onion
- ½ teaspoon chopped fresh tarragon
- salt and pepper

TO GARNISH:

- 1 pear, cored and sliced
- fresh tarragon

1 In a large salad bowl, mix the lettuce with the celery, red pepper, walnuts, grapes, pear and smoked chicken.
2 Mix the yogurt with the mayonnaise, cucumber, onion and tarragon, blending well. Add salt and pepper to taste.
3 Just before serving, spoon the dressing over the salad ingredients and toss well to mix.
4 Garnish with slices of pear and a few sprigs of fresh tarragon.

Serves 8
Preparation time: 25 minutes

**Kcal 116; KJ 485; Protein 11 (g)
Fat 5 (g); CHO 6 (g)**

VARIATION

Soured Cream and Courgette Dressing

Make the dressing by mixing 2 tablespoons low-fat soured cream with 2 tablespoons low-fat mayonnaise, 1 tablespoon grated courgette or cucumber, 2 teaspoons grated onion and salt and pepper to taste.

Serves 8
Preparation time: 7 minutes

**Kcal 75; KJ 314; Protein 3 (g)
Fat 5 (g); CHO 5 (g)**

Mushroom, Courgette and Tomato Salad

- 6 large mushrooms, sliced
- 4 courgettes, thinly sliced
- 4 tomatoes, skinned and quartered
- 1 teaspoon chopped fresh basil
- 1 bunch of cress, trimmed and divided into strips
- Citrus Dressing (see below), to serve

1 Combine the mushrooms, courgettes and tomatoes in a salad bowl and sprinkle with the basil.
2 Arrange the sprigs of cress round the edge of the salad. Serve with Citrus Dressing.

Serves 4
Preparation time: 10 minutes

Kcal 25; KJ 107; Protein 2 (g) Fat 0; CHO 4 (g)

Citrus Dressing

- 100 ml/3½ fl oz fresh orange juice
- 2 tablespoons fresh lime juice
- 1 tablespoon fresh lemon juice
- 1 teaspoon cider vinegar
- ½ teaspoon granular low-calorie sweetener
- pepper

Put all the ingredients into a screwtop jar and shake well.

Coleslaw

- 500 g/1 lb white cabbage, shredded
- 125 g/4 oz carrots, grated
- 1 onion, sliced
- Lemon Yogurt Dressing (see page 9)
- 1 tablespoon finely chopped fresh parsley

1 Mix the cabbage with the carrot and onion in a large bowl.

2 Add the Lemon Yogurt Dressing and toss vigorously. Garnish with the parsley and chill until ready to serve

Serves 4
Preparation time: 10 minutes

Kcal 73; KJ 306; Protein 5 (g)
Fat 1 (g); CHO 13 (g)

Desserts and Ice Creams

French Apple Flan

There is no need to grease tins when cooking this type of pastry because of the high fat content of the dough. In some other recipes the tins may need to be greased.

150 g/5 oz plain flour
50 g/2 oz butter
50 g/2 oz caster sugar
1 egg and 1 egg white, beaten together
few drops vanilla essence

1 kg/2 lb cooking apples, peeled, cored and thinly sliced and puréed
2 red-skinned dessert apples, thinly sliced
50 g/2 oz caster sugar
4 tablespoons apricot jam
juice of ½ lemon

1 To make the pâte sucrée, sift the flour on to a cool work surface. Make a well in the centre and add the butter, sugar, egg and egg white and vanilla essence. Using the fingertips of one hand, work these ingredients together, then draw in the flour. Knead lightly until smooth, then cover and chill for 1 hour.

2 Roll out the pastry very thinly on a floured work surface and use to line a 25 cm/ 10 inch fluted flan ring. Fill the case generously with the apple purée, then arrange an overlapping layer of apples on top. Sprinkle with the sugar. Bake in a preheated oven, 190°C (375°F), Gas Mark 5, for 35–40 minutes.

3 Meanwhile, heat the jam with the lemon juice, then strain and brush over the apples. Serve hot or cold.

Serves 10
Preparation time: 15 minutes, plus chilling
Cooking time: 35–40 minutes
Oven temperature: 190°C (375°F), Gas Mark 5

Kcal 211; KJ 889; Protein 3 (g); Fat 5 (g); CHO 41 (g)

Kiwi Fruit Meringue Cake

- vegetable oil, for brushing
- 3 egg whites
- 1 teaspoon cream of tartar
- 75 g/3 oz caster sugar
- 1 teaspoon cornflour
- 4 kiwi fruit, peeled and thinly sliced

1 Cover a baking sheet with non-stick baking paper or foil and lightly brush with oil.

2 Half whisk the egg whites. Add the cream of tartar and whisk until very stiff. Whisk in the sugar a little at a time. Finally whisk in the cornflour.

3 Spoon the meringue mixture on to the prepared baking sheet and lightly flatten into an 18 cm/7 inch circle with a palette knife, building up the edge of the meringue slightly.

4 Bake the meringue in a preheated oven, 110°C (225°F), Gas Mark ¼, for about 1½ hours, until set. Remove from the oven and allow to cool, then carefully peel off the lining paper.

5 Transfer the meringue to a serving plate and arrange the kiwi fruit on top. Serve on the day of making.

Serves 4

Preparation time: 10 minutes
Cooking time: about 1½ hours
Oven temperature: 110°C (225°F), Gas Mark ¼

**Kcal 120; KJ 506; Protein 3 (g)
Fat 0 (g); CHO 28 (g)**

Curd Cheese Hearts

- 250 g/8 oz low-fat cottage cheese, sieved
- artificial sweetener, to taste
- 150 ml/¼ pint natural yogurt
- 2 egg whites
- 1 tablespoon brandy

TO DECORATE:

- tiny fresh vine leaves (if available)
- small clusters of black grapes

1 Mix the cottage cheese with a little sweetener to taste (if you don't have a very sweet tooth, this may not be necessary). Blend in the yogurt.

2 Whisk the egg whites until stiff but not dry. Fold lightly but thoroughly into the cheese mixture, together with the brandy.

3 Line 4 small perforated heart-shaped moulds with clean muslin. Spoon the cheese mixture into the lined moulds and cover with another layer of muslin.

4 Place the moulds on a tray or baking sheet with a rim, and chill for 6–8 hours. The excess liquid should have drained away from the cheese, and the moulds should be firm enough to turn out.

5 Unmould the hearts and decorate with vine leaves and clusters of grapes.

Serves 4

Preparation time: 30 minutes, plus chilling

**Kcal 94; KJ 396; Protein 11 (g)
Fat 3 (g); CHO 5 (g)**

Orange Diet Cheesecake

- 40 g/1½ oz low-fat spread, softened
- 8 digestive biscuits, crushed
- 125 g/4 oz very low fat cottage cheese
- 4 tablespoons skimmed milk
- 375 g/12 oz quark
- 3 tablespoons orange juice
- grated rind of 2 oranges
- artificial liquid sweetener, to taste
- 2 eggs, separated
- 15 g/½ oz powdered gelatine
- 3 tablespoons water
- 4 large oranges

1 Lightly grease an 18 cm/7 inch loose-bottomed cake tin with a little of the low-fat spread. Mix the remaining spread with the biscuit crumbs. Spoon evenly over the base of the cake tin and press down firmly with the back of a wooden spoon.

2 Meanwhile, purée the cottage cheese and milk in a blender until smooth. Mix together the quark, cottage cheese mixture, orange juice and rind and artificial sweetener to taste. Beat the egg yolks into the mixture, one at a time, beating well after each addition.

3 Sprinkle the gelatine over the water in a small heatproof bowl and leave for a few minutes until spongy. Place the bowl in a saucepan of hot water and stir over a very gentle heat until dissolved. Allow to cool slightly, then stir into the cheese mixture. Chill in the refrigerator until thick and just beginning to set. Whisk the egg whites stiffly, then fold them into the cheese mixture, using a large metal spoon.

4 Pour the cheese mixture over the crumb base. Smooth the surface and chill in the refrigerator for about 5 hours until set.

5 Peel and divide the oranges into segments. Decorate the top edge of the cheesecake with the larger, better-looking slices and sprinkle the centre with the reserved rind.

Serves 10
Preparation time: 15 minutes, plus setting time

Kcal 128; KJ 536; Protein 10 (g); Fat 5 (g); CHO 11 (g)

Strawberry Diet Cheesecake

For a Strawberry Diet Cheesecake use the grated rind of 2 lemons and 3 tablespoons lemon juice instead of oranges and decorate with 125 g/4 oz hulled and sliced strawberries. Other alternative toppings are 3 chopped pineapple rings or 75 g/3 oz halved and seeded grapes.

Chocolate Soufflé

Even a drop of egg yolk will prevent egg whites from rising, so separate eggs very carefully, one at a time.

- vegetable oil, for greasing
- 75 ml/3 fl oz fresh orange juice
- 75 g/3 oz sugar
- 4 large egg whites
- 25 g/1 oz unsweetened cocoa powder
- 2 tablespoons orange liqueur
- 125 g/4 oz low-fat vanilla ice cream, softened

1 Grease 6 cups with the oil.
2 In a small saucepan, heat the orange juice and sugar for 3–4 minutes over medium-high heat, stirring occasionally, until the mixture has a syrupy consistency. Remove from the heat.
3 In a large bowl, beat the egg whites until stiff; stop before dry peaks form. Pour the syrup over the egg whites and beat for 2 minutes. Add the cocoa and liqueur and beat only until well mixed. Pour into the prepared cups. Bake in a preheated oven, 150°C (300°F), Gas Mark 2, for 2 minutes, or until the

soufflés are puffed. Do not overbake, or the soufflés will become tough.
4 To serve, spoon 2 tablespoons softened vanilla ice cream into the centre of each soufflé. Serve immediately.

Serves 6
Preparation time: 10 minutes
Cooking time: 12 minutes
Oven temperature: 150°C (300°F), Gas Mark 2

**Kcal 116; KJ 489; Protein 3 (g)
Fat 3 (g); CHO 19 (g)**

Summer Pudding

This classic English pudding is made with a selection of summer soft fruits which you can vary as you choose. The addition of gelatine makes the serving of the pudding much easier. Use one of the softer, lighter types of brown bread for this recipe.

- 250 g/8 oz red and white currants
- 125 g/4 oz blackcurrants
- 125 g/4 oz raspberries
- 125 g/4 oz loganberries
- 125 g/4 oz strawberries
- 125 g/4 oz cherries, blueberries or culti- vated blackberries
- 1 tablespoon clear honey
- 1 sachet gelatine (optional)
- margarine, for greasing
- 8 x 1 cm/½ inch thick slices brown bread, crusts removed (see below)

1 Place all the fruit in a large saucepan (it must not be aluminium or cast iron) with the honey and cook very gently for 2–3 minutes, just long enough to soften the fruit and allow the juices to run a little.
2 Sprinkle the gelatine over and stir it in very carefully, trying not to crush the fruit.
3 Line a lightly greased 1.2 litre/2 pint pudding basin with three-quarters of the bread, trimming the slices to fit, making certain that all the surfaces are completely covered and the base has an extra thick layer.
4 Spoon in all the fruit, reserving 2 tablespoons of the juice in case the bread is not completely coloured by the fruit when the pudding is turned out. Cover with the remaining bread. Lay a plate or saucepan lid that will fit inside the rim of the bowl on top and place a 1 kg/2 lb weight on top. Chill for 10–12 hours.
5 Turn out and cut into wedges to serve.

Serves 4
Preparation time: 30 minutes, plus chilling
Cooking time: 3 minutes

Kcal 150; KJ 620; Protein 5 (g)
Fat 1 (g); CHO 30 (g)

Strawberries with Blackcurrant Sauce

- 250 g/8 oz blackcurrants, trimmed
- 2 tablespoons clear honey
- 3 tablespoons red wine
- 375 g/12 oz strawberries, hulled and halved
- small sprigs of fresh redcurrants, to decorate

1 Put the blackcurrants into a pan with the honey and red wine; stir well, then simmer gently for about 5 minutes or until the natural fruit juices are released.
2 Pour the blackcurrants and their liquid into a food processor or blender and purée until fairly smooth – the sauce should still have some texture. Leave to cool.
3 Arrange the halved strawberries on a serving dish and spoon the blackcurrant sauce beside them.
4 Decorate with the sprigs of fresh redcurrants and serve.

Serves 4
Preparation time: 25 minutes, plus cooling
Cooking time: 5 minutes

**Kcal 85; Kj 370; Protein 1 (g)
Fat 0 (g); CHO 20 (g)**

Stuffed Figs

- 12 ripe fresh figs, preferably purple ones
- 3 tablespoons ground almonds
- 125 g/4 oz fresh raspberries
- 1 tablespoon clear honey
- 4 vine leaves, soaked in warm water and dried, to serve

1 Snip off any excess stalk from each fig. Make a criss-cross cut down from the stalk end and carefully ease the cut open.

2 Mix the ground almonds with the fresh raspberries and honey.

3 Place a vine leaf, spread out flat, on each serving plate. Arrange 3 figs on top of each one and fill with the raspberry and almond purée.

Serves 4
Preparation time: 10–15 minutes

**Kcal 4; KJ 135; Protein 4 (g)
Fat 5 (g); CHO 20 (g)**

Spiced Pears

- 4 large firm pears
- ½ lemon
- 16 cloves
- ½ cinnamon stick

- 300 ml/½ pint red wine
- 2 tablespoons redcurrant jelly
- 4 orange slices
- 4 small fresh bay leaves, to decorate

1 Peel the pears, leaving the stalks intact. Rub them all over with the lemon half to prevent discoloration.

2 Stud each pear with 4 cloves. Stand them upright in a pan and add the cinnamon stick, wine and sufficient water just to cover the pears.

3 Bring to the boil and simmer gently until the pears are just tender. Leave to cool in the cooking liquid.

4 Put 2 tablespoons of the cooking liquid into a small pan with the redcurrant jelly. Bubble briskly for about 1 minute until the jelly has dissolved.

5 Place an orange slice on each of 4 small plates. Drain the pears with a slotted spoon, and sit one on top of each orange slice.

6 Spoon a little of the redcurrant glaze over each pear and decorate with a bay leaf.

Serves 4
Preparation time: 20 minutes
Cooking time: about 16 minutes

Kcal 86; KJ 360; Protein 1 (g); Fat 0 (g); CHO 22 (g)

Peach Granita

- 375 g/12 oz fresh ripe peaches
- 150 ml/¼ pint dry white wine
- 150 ml/¼ pint fresh orange juice
- 2 egg whites

1 Nick the stalk end of each peach. Plunge into a bowl of boiling water for 45 seconds, then slide off the skins. Halve the fruit, removing the stones, and chop the flesh roughly.
2 Put the peach flesh into a pan with the white wine and orange juice. Simmer gently for 5 minutes.
3 Blend the peaches and the liquid in a food processor or blender until smooth. Cool.
4 Pour into a shallow freezer container and freeze until the granita is slushy around the edges, then tip into a bowl and break up the ice crystals.
5 Whisk the egg whites until stiff but not dry. Fold lightly but thoroughly into the partly-frozen granita, return to the container and freeze until firm.

Serves 4
Preparation time: 20–25 minutes, plus freezing
Cooking time: 5 minutes

**Kcal 70; Kj 290; Protein 2 (g)
Fat 1 (g); CHO 9 (g)**

Yogurt-Fruit Cup

This offers a new twist to a back-to-basics favourite. You'll like the fragrant touch of cardamom.

- 1 x 500 g/1 lb can sliced peaches or pears in fruit juice, drained
- 475 ml/16 fl oz low-fat vanilla yogurt
- 2 tablespoons finely chopped toasted almonds
- ½ teaspoon ground cinnamon

Divide the fruit among 6 small dessert bowls. Top with yogurt and sprinkle lightly with nuts and cardamom. Serve immediately.

Serves 6
Preparation time: 10 minutes

**Kcal 124; Kj 526; Protein 4 (g)
Fat 3 (g); CHO 23 (g)**

Melon Ice Cream

- 1 large melon (Ogen or Charentais)
- 300 ml/½ pint natural yogurt

1 Halve the melon and scoop out all the seeds. Scoop the melon flesh into a food processor or blender and work until smooth.
2 Mix the melon purée with the yogurt.
3 Transfer the melon and yogurt mixture to a shallow freezer container, and freeze until firm.
4 Serve the melon ice cream in scoops.

Serves 4
Preparation time: 20–25 minutes, plus freezing

Kcal 90; Kj 380; Protein 5 (g); Fat 0 (g); CHO 16 (g)

Blackcurrant and Orange Ice Cream

- 250 g/8 oz blackcurrants, hulled if fresh, thawed if frozen
- finely grated rind of 1 orange
- 6 tablespoons fresh unsweetened orange juice
- 6–8 mint leaves
- 4 tablespoons soft light brown sugar
- 300 ml/½ pint natural low-fat yogurt
- 2 eggs, separated

1 Reserve a few blackcurrants for decoration, if wished, and place the remainder in a food processor or blender with the orange rind and juice, the mint leaves, sugar, yogurt and egg yolks. Process until smooth, then strain through a fine sieve. Transfer the mixture to a freezerproof bowl and freeze for about 1 hour or until half frozen.

2 Remove the mixture from the freezer and beat well. Whisk the egg whites stiffly and fold into the mixture. Return to the freezer for 1 further hour or until half frozen again, then beat again and return to the freezer for 1 hour or until firm.

3 Transfer the ice cream to the main part of the refrigerator for 20–30 minutes before serving.

4 Serve in chilled individual glasses, decorated with any reserved black-currants.

Serves 6
Preparation time: 15 mintues, plus freezing

Kcal 135; Kj 585; Protein 8 (g) Fat 3 (g); CHO 22 (g)

Whole Strawberry Ice Cream

- 3 egg yolks
- 1 tablespoon redcurrant jelly
- 1 tablespoon red vermouth
- 300 ml/½ pint natural yogurt
- 375 g/12 oz ripe strawberries, hulled
- 4–6 strawberries, with stalks, halved, to decorate

1 Put the egg yolks into a blender or food processor with the redcurrant jelly, vermouth, yogurt and half the strawberries and blend until smooth.
2 Transfer the mixture to a shallow freezerproof container, and freeze until the ice cream starts to harden around the edges.
3 Tip the ice cream into a bowl and beat to break up the ice crystals. Chop the remaining strawberries and mix into the half-frozen ice cream. Return to the container and freeze until quite firm.
4 Scoop the ice cream into stemmed glasses and decorate each one with strawberry halves.

Serves 4
Preparation time: 25 minutes, plus freezing

Kcal 126; Kj 525; Protein 7 (g) Fat 5 (g); CHO 14 (g)

Recipe Photographers:
Octopus Publishing Group Ltd
/Philip Dowell /Gus Filgate
/Graham Kirk /Diana Miller
/Hilary Moore /Vernon Morgan
/James Murphy /Clive Streeter
Jacket Photographer:
Simon Smith
Jacket Home Economist: